SURVIVING AN AUTO ACCIDENT

A Guide to Your Physical, Emotional and Economic Recovery

by

Robert Saperstein, J.D. & Dana Saperstein, Ph.D.

Pathfinder Publishing of California

Ventura, California

SURVIVING AN AUTO ACCIDENT

Published by:
Pathfinder Publishing of California
458 Dorothy Avenue
Ventura, CA 93003
(805) 642-9278

Library of Congress Cataloging-in-Publication Data
Saperstein, Robert, 1958
   Surviving an auto accident : a guide to your physical, emotional, and economic recovery / Robert Saperstein & Dana Saperstein.
   P. cm.
   Includes index.
   ISBN 0-934793-55-7 : $12.95
   1. Traffic accident victims. 2. Traffic accidents. 3. Insurance, Automobile. 4. Insurance, Automobile—Law and legislation. 5. Liability for traffic accidents. I. Saperstein, Dana, 1955- . II. Title.
HE5614.S34 1044
363.12'5—dc20   94-2303
                                     CIP

DEDICATION

This book is dedicated to the millions of accident victims whose lives are irreversibly altered by their accident experience. We wish you well and Godspeed on your road to health.

DISCLAIMER

This publication is designed to provide accurate and authoritative information in regard to the subject matter covered. It is sold with the understanding that the publisher is not engaged in rendering legal, security, psychological, medical, or other professional services. If expert assistance or counseling is needed, the services of a competent professional should be sought.

ACKNOWLEDGMENTS

We have many people to thank for their help, support and input in completing this project. Together, we'd like to thank:

Eugene Wheeler, our editor and publisher at Pathfinder Publishing. Without his support and belief in this book it would not have found its way into your hands. Thanks also to Kathleen Sublette, Kathy Stinson and Eugenie Wheeler of Pathfinder Publishing.

Dr. Allen Thomashefsky. Without his knowledge, expertise and encouragement this book would not have been possible.

Susan Saperstein for her patience and meticulous attention to detail in reading through the manuscript several times. With two small children, quiet time is a premium. Thanks for spending some of it on this book.

Catherine Weissenberg for her support and review of information contained in the manuscript. Her common sense approach helped make the book much more accessible and understandable.

Dana's many clients whose accident experiences helped shape this book. And the many other professionals who shared their knowledge and experience in working with accident victims.

CONTENTS

INTRODUCTION

Reading this guide before you have a car accident may be best, but is not necessary. The guide can benefit you as an accident victim anytime after an accident, but preferably as soon after the time of the crash as possible. Ideally, every driving student should read this guide or a similar one during driver education. If you had an accident some time ago, it would be wise to read this to ensure that you've learned as much as you can from the experience, as unfortunately, it's possible you might have another accident.

Dana Saperstein:

If someone had tried to convince me that a relatively minor car accident *could and would* profoundly change my life I would have laughed. It sounds melodramatic, but the few moments it took for the other driver to run a stop sign and smash into the side of my car changed the shape and direction of my personal and professional life more dramatically than perhaps any other event in my adult life — so much for career planning and foresight.

This accident happened in the summer of 1988. I was in a quiet driving daze coming home from work on a Friday afternoon, looking forward to a couple days away from my office. By the time I realized the other car wasn't going to stop, it was too late to do anything but hang on tight and wait for the glass to settle. The sudden, violent intrusion of a ton of metal coming at me took my breath away. In an instant, I was yanked from the cozy warmth of my family-weekend fantasies and plunged out of control into an icy pool of fear and helplessness. I had my seat belt on and we were both only going about 25 miles per hour, but in those few seconds, just before and during impact, I wasn't sure I would live through it.

As our cars skidded together I could see the other driver's face clearly, but then on impact it looked like her head cracked into a million pieces as my windshield shattered. Her car struck the forward passenger side of my car; the crushing of metal to metal, the screeching tires, and the exploding glass were deafening. I was thrown at a diagonal against my shoulder-strap, we bounced some, and then it was over. The quiet was such a contrast. I half expected my car doors and hubcaps to fall off and my tires to deflate like in a cartoon car crash.

Once I realized I was okay and I saw the other driver climb from her car on her own, my heart slowly sank back into my chest. I could feel a noxious mix of fear, anger, and confusion stewing in my stomach. I really wanted to scream at the stupidity of this woman. WHY DIDN'T SHE STOP? HOW COULD SHE DO THIS TO ME? WHAT DID I DO TO DESERVE THIS? I knew there was nothing she could say or do that would undo the damage and take away my rage. As best I could, I swallowed my anger. All she could say was she didn't see the stop sign.

I thought a phone call to my insurance company would pretty much be the end of the experience. After dinner my lower back started getting stiff and tender. I thought I was just tired. We had a new baby and a two-year-old, sometimes a good night's sleep was hard to find. Back spasms woke me up in the middle of the night. Even then, I didn't connect my pain to the accident. I took a muscle relaxant and figured I would take it easy for a few days.

By the middle of the next week my lower back ached continuously. Without knowing that I had been in a wreck, a client of mine recommended I see a physician who happened to be an accident and sports injury specialist. It wasn't until I was sitting on this physician's examining table, telling him about the craziness of the past week, that I realized the accident was the likely cause of my pain. I had been thrown forward and sideways abruptly, at an abnormal angle. The physician said car accidents commonly cause this type of soft tissue injury, that I probably damaged the tendons and/or ligaments that provide the supporting structure of my lower back.

It took 13 months before my back finally felt healthy. I progressed through a regime of physical therapy, massage, chiropractic adjustment, acupuncture, and finally, a series of proliferant injections. If I hadn't been lucky enough to find a physician who recognized the necessity of a multi-dimensional approach in treating accident injuries, I might still be struggling with my back.

During this time, the same physician invited me to shift my psychotherapy practice and work within his treatment group. My focus would be on the psychological trauma associated with automobile accidents. He was finding, over and over, that a significant factor in the physical healing process was the emotional health or dis-ease of his patients. And many mental health experts were coming to view the impact of everyday violence and trauma in a different light; they were finding that relatively common events, such as violent crimes, plane crashes, natural disasters like hurricanes and earthquakes, and even **automobile accidents** can inflict significant psychological damage. I decided to move my therapy practice. As I started working with people involved in automobile wrecks, and thought more about my own terrifying experience, I began to realize how emotionally significant and powerful even a relatively minor accident can be.

Meanwhile, I was still picking up the economic pieces of my own accident. Even though the woman who hit me admitted fault, I couldn't settle with her insurance company until I knew the extent of my injury and what it was going to take to get well. Her insurance company assured me that once my condition stabilized, we would come to some mutual agreement. But many of my clients were having trouble working with insurance claims representatives, attorneys, and employers (in instances of on-the-job auto accidents). Often my days were filled with listening to my clients' stories (you will find some of them in the pages that follow) of confusion and frustration in working with the accident recovery "system."

Many crash victim clients with whom I worked felt just as victimized by the "system" that is supposedly designed to help them heal as they did from the accident itself. Note that the term "accident victim" is meant inclusively, that is, to encompass all those involved in automobile accidents whether they were legally "at fault" or not. Perhaps a more accurate term would be "accident survivor" but somehow that sounds too formidable. Whether it was dealing with the physical wounds, emotional upset, economic and legal hardship, or more likely some combination of all three, most of these clients were not prepared to handle the giant-sized monkey wrench thrown into their lives. Even more troublesome was that there really was no place for them or me to get accurate, reliable guidance to help them through the recovery system maze.

At this point, I have spent hundreds of hours counseling the victims of car crashes. We have learned together, from each other. This book is born out of the tears of fear, anger, confusion and frustration of those victims who never expected they would have to deal with, nor were prepared for the enormity of the task of healing from the physical, economic, and emotional trauma of a car accident. Rob (my co-author and brother) and I also spent many hours interviewing some of the astonishingly diverse collection of professionals whose livelihood depends on accident victims. Rob and I have drawn upon the experience of hundreds of victims and professionals to make this information available in the distilled form you now find.

Surviving an Auto Accident is meant to empower you with knowledge and the courage to take responsibility for your own healing process and to accept nothing less than physical, economic, and emotional recovery from your automobile accident. My overriding hope is that you will use the information contained in this book to make healthy, responsible choices for yourself. You cannot change the perspective of all the professionals with whom you interact, but you can choose whom and how you pay to get well. I also hope and expect that many professionals will find this information useful both in better understanding the full impact an automobile accident has on an individual's life, and in broadening their own compassion and ability to assist accident victims in their recovery.

Rob Saperstein:

I was about six-years-old when I was in my first and most serious car cash. My Mom was driving a bunch of us to the beach in our monster 1960 Chevy Impala. I was sitting in the back with my friends and my brother Dana was riding shotgun. We were only a half-mile from the beach when a car ran a stop sign and we ran into it. My Mom just didn't see it coming across our path until it was in front of us.

Wearing seat belts was practically unheard of in those dark ages, but my friends and I in the backseat had a big canvas beach raft stuffed across our knees. In what may have been the first successful test of an airbag-like device, our faces just bounced off the raft on impact.

In the front seat, Dana wasn't quite so lucky. As he slid forward, the metal glovebox door flew open and sliced across his knee. When I saw the blood dripping down his leg, I was sure he was going to die. Bordering on hysteria, I asked him over and over if he was okay. At first I couldn't hear his response because I was hypnotized by the blood. I was finally convinced he would make it when, in his loving way, he told me to shut-up and leave him alone.

Because I didn't have to worry about getting our car fixed or paying for Dana's medical bills, what stuck with me was how terrifying the experience was. One minute we were crazy with anticipation over a day at the beach and the next I was sure my older brother was going to bleed to death in front of me. Now, almost thirty years later, all I need to do is close my eyes and imagine the blood—the fear wells up in my stomach like it was yesterday.

As I worked on this book I tried to keep this experience foremost in my mind. I wanted to make sure I wrote in a voice that showed respect for the recentering that everyone involved in a car accident must go through. Whether from physical injuries, economic hardship, emotional trauma, or from some combination of the three, healing from a car accident takes time, patience, and determination. As Dana said, being involved in an automobile accident is an unexpected and difficult curve to handle even in the best of circumstances. By writing with a compassionate, empowering, confident intent, I hope you, the accident victim reading this, are better able to develop and draw on your own and other resources in a way that best suits your individual needs.

Whether it concerns your body, your mind, or your pocketbook, the more you know about the recovery process, the more you are able to identify and articulate what you need. *Surviving an Auto Accident* is designed to jumpstart you on this learning curve—you may not find all the answers in this book, but you should learn enough to avoid the common pitfalls. You will learn enough to know the right questions to ask along the way.

As Dana mentioned, this book is not ours alone. It is a product of many people, and their experiences. I'm deeply grateful that they cared enough to share their personal stories. Many of these "war stories" are woven into the body of the book and help put the factual details in a more intimate, understandable context. Although every accident is unique, these real life experiences will help you make good decisions for yourself.

In some instances the stories are related in the first person, just as they were told to us. In others, the stories are condensed and retold in the third-person. In all cases, the experiences are real although pseudonyms were used to insure confidentiality.

Finally, from my perspective as an attorney, I believe that self-help is not only about getting good information but also about acting in your own best interests, for the sake of your own recovery. With this book, you will learn how "the system" works. Your job is to take this information, add a strong, questioning voice, a desire to become well again, and the unique factors of your accident. Given that combination you can create a much healthier, more satisfying healing process for yourself.

January 1994

Santa Barbara, California

Chapter 1

THE ACCIDENT EXPERIENCE

WHAT'S THE "PROCESS?"

Car accidents occur more frequently than murders, rapes, robberies, assaults, burglaries, and most thefts combined. More than once a second, just about every time your heart beats, there is a violent motor vehicle accident in the United States. In 1992, vehicle accidents injured five million people and killed close to 40,000. Nearly one half, or 19,000 of these killed, and 355,000 injured, were involved in alcohol-related vehicle crashes. All in all, over 5,000,000 Americans each year wish they had left home a little earlier, stayed at the office a few minutes later, or stopped for gas along the way — anything to have avoided being in the wrong place, at the wrong time.

Rob

I was driving home late one evening on a relatively quiet two-lane city street. I remember trying to decide whether to eat pizza or a burger for dinner when an oncoming car swerved out of place into my lane. It happened so fast, the other car was so close, there was no way I could avoid the crash. All I could do is slam on my brakes and wait out the terror.

Once the glass settled, I looked for blood and tried to sense where the pain was worst. I remember thinking this must be a nightmare, that in a few moments I'll wake up, shaken, but at home in my own bed.

Unfortunately, I was awake and the accident was quite real. The front of my car looked like a crumpled aluminum can. With luck, it would only cost a few thousand dollars and take a few weeks to repair.

Reparing the damage to my car wouldn't have been too difficult if my neck hadn't felt like it was locked in a nail-faced vice. Bolts of lightning white pain shot out from the base of my neck whenever I moved. Sleep, aspirin, a hot bath — nothing seemed to dissolve my headache. Just getting out of bed the morning after the accident was like climbing Mount Everest.

A few days after the accident I was feeling even more unnerved. I was anxious, I hadn't had a comfortable night of sleep since the accident, and I was worried about money. My head swirled with thousands of questions and I had little idea where to look or who to trust for concrete answers. Did I get all the information I needed at the scene of the accident? How do I get my car fixed? What does my insurance policy cover and what does the other driver's policy cover? Do I need an attorney and if so how do I find one? The trip to the emergency room alone cost $1000. How and when do I get reimbursed for all the medical bills? Will my whiplash heal in a month or six months? Should I see a chiropractor even though my physician did not rec-

*ommend it? When will I stop feeling so jumpy and
tense? Will I ever feel safe or relaxed in a car again?
When will my life return to normal?*

The questions are dizzying; each one leads to ten
more. If you are like most accident victims, all you really
want to do is crawl under your bed-covers and let your pain
and confusion subside. If you have not experienced it, it is
hard to imagine how disruptive and life-altering an accident can be. Unraveling all the questions and restoring a
life knocked askew by an automobile accident takes some
time. Recovery is a process, not an event. The impact, the
crumpling of the protective shell of metal and glass, marks
the beginning of an intensely personal struggle for physical, emotional, and economic recovery which may take a
lifetime.

ANATOMY OF THE ACCIDENT RECOVERY MAZE

Although every accident is unique — your particular
circumstances and needs dictate the details of your recovery — there is a distinct framework to the recovery process.
In general, the physical, economic, and emotional resolution of an accident proceeds through the following characteristic stages.

THE ACCIDENT INVESTIGATION

Immediately after most major accidents, the police
conduct an investigation. The thoroughness of their in-
quiry depends on the circumstances and severity of the
wreck. Most big cities no longer send police officers to
wrecks unless they involve injuries. You should also prepare your own accident report as described in Chapter 2.

When the insurance companies are notified, they
begin an independent investigation, although they do rely
heavily on the findings of the official police report. If

insurance claims are filed, the company claims representatives interview witnesses and those involved in the accident, review the police report, and possibly consult with accident experts to determine the exact cause of the crash. Economic resolution usually cannot be completed until the insurance companies decide who is to blame for the accident.

AUTOMOTIVE REPAIRS

In general, you are responsible for arranging for your car repairs. The ultimate responsibility for the cost of repairs depends on who is to blame for the accident, and the type of liability and property damage insurance carried by those involved.

In 1991, the USAA insurance company reported that the average vehicle repair cost was approximately $2,000. Since the federal bumper safety requirements were relaxed in 1982, even the most minor accident can cause considerable damage. For example, after a five mph rear bumper crash test the repair cost for the 1990 Ford Escort LX was $1,404.

PHYSICAL TREATMENT

While the investigation proceeds, you arrange for the medical care you need. Depending on the type of insurance coverage you have, medical expenses may not be paid for you until an insurance settlement is complete. Medical expenses account for about 70% of the economic cost of most accidents. The average cost per claim for physical treatment in 1987 was about $4,600 (Rand Corporation study). Your actual cost will depend on the severity of your injuries and the particular treatment you elect.

Soft tissue damage is by far the most common type of accident injury. A wide variety of treatment methodologies are available for this type of injury. Mistakes made in treating soft tissue injuries can result in chronic pain and lifelong disabilities.

PSYCHOLOGICAL TREATMENT

A motor vehicle accident is a traumatic experience. Not only does it damage cars and bodies but it can take a psychological toll as well. Psychological treatment is often a necessary component of a comprehensive rehabilitation program.

Emotional healing is important because it is the area of recovery most likely to be overlooked or taken for granted. The potential impact of the trauma of an automobile accident on emotional well-being cannot be overstated. The psychological wounds inflicted during an automobile accident are as real and as treatable as physical injuries. Often, until emotional trauma is addressed, physical healing is impeded.

THE INSURANCE CLAIMS PROCESS

Even relatively minor accidents can be economically devastating. As mentioned, just fixing a bumper can cost several hundred dollars. A series of spinal x-rays, a must for whiplash victims, can run over $500. Meanwhile, you might lose several days, weeks, or months of wages while recovering from your injuries. It is unlikely that your wallet can easily absorb this kind of economic shock. This is why drivers pay so much for automobile insurance. Unfortunately, the system supposedly designed to help you, the accident victim, is not always "user friendly."

The path of your economic recovery—the insurance claims process—follows three distinct courses. The first is working with your insurance company as it defends claims brought against you for damage which you caused. In most cases, there is not much for you to do in this scenario other than cooperate with your insurance company and its attorneys, unless you have evidence that supports your innocence.

The second course is making a claim on your own policy to pay for aspects of your own personal and property damages. The amount of money available depends on the type of insurance coverage you have purchased. If you have the appropriate coverage, your own insurance policy will pay to repair your vehicle and for some portion of your medical expenses. In some no-fault states, you might also be reimbursed for lost wages through your own insurer.

The third course, which gives rise to the vast majority of automobile accident personal injury lawsuits, is making a claim against the other driver's insurance policy. In general, a settlement from another driver's insurer is paid in one lump sum. In exchange for the cash settlement, you give up all future rights to make a claim for damages resulting from the accident.

You may also decide to hire an attorney to help negotiate the dollar value of the settlement with the other driver's insurer. It will be difficult to settle your claim until your injuries stabilize, enabling you to make an accurate estimate of treatment costs. Negotiating a settlement takes time. As a rule, the larger the claim, the longer it takes to settle and the more likely a lawsuit will be necessary. About 80% of all claims are settled without filing a lawsuit.

THE PERSONAL INJURY LAWSUIT

If a case cannot be settled, usually because the parties do not agree on the cause of the accident and/or the dollar value of the damages, a lawsuit may be filed. Once this occurs, the process often becomes very antagonistic and time-consuming. The resolution of a lawsuit progresses through a number of stages.

The Lawsuit Discovery Process. Both sides of the lawsuit try to find out as much as they can about the accident, the victims, and their claimed injuries. Witnesses and accident experts are integral components of the case at this stage. During the discovery process, the medical, psychological, and economic history of the victims are thoroughly reviewed. This can be an uncomfortable and disheartening aspect of your own recovery.

Throughout this pretrial phase of the lawsuit, the lawyers from both sides, based on their experience and the details of the case, will try to negotiate a settlement. Over 95% of all cases settle before trial.

Arbitration and settlement conference. Many insurance policies and court systems require that the case go before an impartial arbitrator before going to trial. In other situations, lawyers for both parties meet with the judge assigned to the case for an informal, pre-trial settlement conference. Again, many cases settle during arbitration or as a result of these pre-trial conferences.

Trial. If the parties cannot come to some agreement, off to court they go. The court (a judge and/or a jury) then decides who and how much if any is to be paid. Only about 1% of accident related personal injury lawsuits actually go to trial.

Appeal. If you are dissatisfied with the outcome of the trial, you may appeal the judgment to the next level of the court system. The appeals court reviews the written record of the case through trial. The appeals court can adjust the monetary damage award, order a new trial, or let the decision stand as it is. This whole process can take many years to complete.

CONCLUSION

The current system available to facilitate your recovery is imperfect at best. Typically, working within the system feels like running through a frustrating maze of bewildering twists and turns. Because of the inexplicable blind curves and innumerable dead ends, the trauma of an automobile accident sometimes turns into a reoccurring nightmare.

The most distressing aspect of many accident recovery experiences is that most of the traumatic aftereffects could be mitigated, if not avoided altogether. Often the only barrier separating you from a safe, passage to health is information. It is no mystery why many of you sincerely feel that your victimization continued long after the broken glass settled. If only you knew what to expect of insurance companies, attorneys, physicians, and the myriad of others involved in the accident recovery maze; if only you knew how best to take control of your physical, economic, and psychological healing, much of your trauma could have been alleviated.

Keep in mind that with this guide in hand, you have taken the first step in understanding the recovery maze. Finding your way to a healthy, wholesome recovery is much more likely.

Chapter 2

THE SCENE OF THE ACCIDENT

YOUR NEXT MOVE CAN MAKE A DIFFERENCE

From the moment the glass settles and crash sounds subside, the recovery process begins. Your actions at the accident scene are your first steps in healing the trauma of the accident. After ensuring your own well-being, establishing a safety zone around the accident scene, and notifying the necessary safety and medical personnel, the few minutes following the accident are the best and perhaps the only time to get the information you need. Witnesses disappear like smoke from a fire and once the cars are moved from their resting spots it might be difficult to accurately reconstruct the accident. You need to take advantage of those moments following the accident to observe everything about the situation.

Obviously, the extent of your physical injuries will influence your actions. If you were knocked unconscious and wake up in the hospital, you didn't have a chance to react at the accident scene. And, if you are seriously hurt you may not be able to do all that we suggest in this chapter. However, the vast majority of accident victims are conscious and functioning immediately following the wreck. As you step from your banged up car you may be upset, scared, and looking for a hole to climb into, or angry and ready to take on the world. On top of the emotional upheaval, you have to deal with an ugly situation. You certainly shouldn't run and hide, so what do you do?

DO NOT LET LOOSE THE EMOTIONAL FLOODGATES

Before you jump out of your car and flail around the accident scene, take a deep breath and try to calm down. One of the more self-destructive things you might do is react to the flood of emotions aroused by the trauma as Paul did:

Paul

It was Friday evening and I was finally on my way home for a few days rest. It had been a terrible work week. It seemed like my boss was on my back continuously from Monday morning until I left Friday evening. My wife promised me a special meal and no responsibility all weekend.

In my daze, I didn't notice a car running the red light until it was too late. There was no time to hit the brakes or turn away, the other car broadsided my passenger side. I was wearing my seat belt but was thrown sideways pretty hard, I could feel the strain in my side and my neck. Most of all, I couldn't believe this had happened. My insides started to boil; by the time I got out of my car there was steam coming out of my ears.

I was screaming in the other driver's face before he had a chance to get out of his car. Unfortunately, he didn't have the sense to stay in his car; instead he got out and tried to talk to me. He was telling me to calm down, that I had no reason to be so angry; all it did was get me more enraged.

Lost Commission
Lost Opportunity to
Gain Clients.

Referred Pain
Tightness in left
shoulder

Anxiety & stress

Don't use "whiplash"

Get Med Reports Sarnia
John

23._____

24._____

25._____

26._____

27._____

28._____

29._____

30._____

31._____

32._____

By the time the police came I had punched him in the face. It must have been quite a scene, two men in suits, him with a bloody nose and me screaming and pushing him around our smashed up cars.

When I realized the police were there, I was able to calm down some but by then it was the other guy's turn to be livid. I spent the next few hours in jail for assaulting this fellow. It turned out that all of the accident witnesses left shortly after I started screaming, but there was no shortage of witnesses to the assault.

Most likely, you will feel scared and shaky because of the drama of the accident and the accompanying adrenaline rush. As much as you might want to, you can't escape the accident scene just yet. Promise yourself that you will find private time to deal with the emotional aspects of the accident later. Over the next few months you will undoubtedly want to cry, rage, and grieve over the incident. For now, as best you can, put your emotions on hold until you get the information you need and until you find a safe place away from the accident scene.

SAFETY ASSESSMENT

Safety must be your initial concern at the accident scene. Assess the situation as though you are a police officer, firefighter, and paramedic. You have to balance a few different safety concerns and perform accident triage: find out who is injured (including yourself), how badly, and decide whether they should be moved to a safer area; determine if there is an ongoing accident danger if the cars and people are left as they sit; and notify all the appropriate authorities. The circumstances of your particular situation should guide your actions.

First, make sure you are okay by taking a moment to let your body talk to you. Where do you hurt and how badly? If you injured your spine, especially your head or neck, the experts say you shouldn't move unless it is too dangerous to stay where you are. Likewise for most other injuries, movement irritates the area and can increase the severity of a wound. So go easy on yourself and minimize your movements until your injuries are stabilized. **Do not be hardheaded about getting medical attention if you need it.** Initially, you must be the judge of how best to care for yourself.

If you aren't seriously hurt, check the passengers in your car and any others involved in the accident. It is important to be prepared for life-threatening injuries, but this chapter is not a replacement for a comprehensive first aid course. People who take the time to learn cardiopulmonary resuscitation (CPR) and emergency first aid save thousands of lives each year. Even if you are not properly trained to administer first aid, you can still quickly evaluate the severity of injuries and get someone to call the paramedics if necessary.

Next, consider clearing the cars from the roadway. Most experts agree that disabled vehicles left in traffic are a significant hazard. Unfortunately, many accident situations worsen shortly after the initial impact by other inattentive drivers running into cars and/or people in the roadway. Certainly, you are not responsible for all the people milling about at the scene, but do your best to make the situation safe.

The police suggest that cars should be moved as soon as possible. Usually, it is only in the more complicated situations that the police need to see the vehicles as they stand to accurately reconstruct the accident. For example, Fort Worth has a city ordinance requiring operative vehicles to be moved off the roadway immediately following a wreck. For minor fender benders and the like, clearing the roadway to eliminate further collision danger is the critical priority. Some insurance experts suggest keeping an inexpensive camera in your car so you can immediately take pictures of the scene but few people are this well prepared. If you feel there is some value in leaving the vehicles until the police arrive, use flares, traffic cones, or other hazard markers to create a safe boundary around the area.

Clearly, you should not have to nor will you be able to do all of the accident triage yourself. In most cases, there will be others around who are willing to help. They may just need direction, so don't hesitate to take charge. While you are lighting flares, ask someone else to call the police, and another person to direct traffic. Oftentimes the first people to stop are witnesses to the accident. If they are performing some safety-related job pertaining to the crash, they are more likely to stick around until you or the police can take their names. To be on the safe side take the tag number of the car of a possible witness in case they decide to leave the scene.

THE POLICE REPORT

Each state has its own legal requirements for reporting traffic accidents. For example, California requires that the police be notified of any accident in which a person is injured, property damage exceeds $500, or if a traffic violation is involved. Be aware that your insurance company may have other notification requirements, particularly if you were hit by an uninsured motorist or are the victim of a hit-and-run accident.

Your state department of motor vehicles may also require notification. Again in California the Department of Motor Vehicles must be notified of any accident causing greater than $500 in damage. Failure to do so within 10 days of the accident can result in the suspension of your driver's license or other fines.

In situations where a police report may not be legally required, such as minor fender benders, the police will still respond when called but it may not be their first priority. Even if it takes the police 20 or 30 minutes to respond, try to be patient. You won't make an ally of a police officer if the first thing you do is give him/her a hard time about how long you have waited. Most police departments will write an accident report at the station house if you contact them within a day or two of the wreck. Note that some experts say these station house reports are of little value since the police were not actually at the scene. Many law enforcement agencies, acknowledging the fact that they often act as surrogate insurance company investigators, now charge a nominal fee for their reports.

As far as the accident report itself, you can imagine that this type of investigation is not necessarily the most exciting or appealing aspect of police work. Even the most conscientious, well-meaning police officer might miss important details and/or omit vital information from the official accident report. Observe the accident scene critically and carefully. Each police department has its own investigative protocol and accident report procedures that you can't be expected to understand. If you are unsatisfied with the police investigation, or don't understand why they are overlooking some seemingly important areas, speak up and ask questions. Police departments have "supplemental accident forms" for a victim to note an error or omission. He/she should ask that a supplemental form be added to the initial report.

Lori

Lori was involved in a multi-car accident at a busy urban intersection. There were hordes of people and cars congesting the scene and the police had their hands full just controlling traffic safety. Lori knew it was important to identify some witnesses but the police didn't seem interested in talking to anyone.

Lori finally found a young woman who claimed to have seen the accident but she refused to give Lori any information; she said she had stopped to make sure no one was hurt but otherwise didn't want to get involved. Lori tried to convince the woman to give the police a statement but she insisted on staying out of the conflict.

Luckily, Lori saw which car the woman was traveling in and that she was temporarily stuck in the fouled up traffic. Lori found a police officer who seemed the least busy with his task and politely presented the situation to him. He was able to convince the young woman of the importance of coming forth as a witness and she finally agreed to provide the police with a statement.

Remember though, the police do not tailor their investigation to what you and the insurance companies will need to settle liability for accident damages. Police investigations are more concerned with controlling criminal behavior and traffic safety. Although the salient details are often identical, the police are not necessarily focused on unearthing the facts central to determining legal liability.

Nevertheless, insurance companies routinely use police reports as the fundamental component of their accident investigation, although witness statements can be equally influential in some cases. Official accident reports are considered accurate, impartial pronouncements of the facts, and perhaps more important to insurers, police investigations and reports save insurance companies millions of dollars in investigative costs. The police report may not capture all the details you need to best present your claim, so to protect your own interests, gather information at the accident scene yourself.

INFORMATION YOU CAN GET TO HELP YOURSELF

Once the scene is relatively safe, don't wait for the police to gather the information you will need later for insurance claims. In one form or another your insurer will need most of the information described below, as will you or your attorney if you make a claim against the other driver's insurance company. Besides having adequate insurance coverage, collecting extensive information at the accident scene will best serve your economic recovery.

Fault determination and thus economic liability (discussed in detail in Chapters 7, 8 and 9) can depend on minor details like whether a driver whose license requires the use of corrective lenses while driving was actually wearing them at the time of the accident. Facts written down immediately, before your memory fades, are less likely to be challenged as uncertain recollections. This doesn't mean everyone will agree on your version, but at least it will portray the facts as you viewed them without the distorting influence of time.

In the rush of the moment you might overlook some important details. See the ready-to-use "Accident Report" forms in Appendix A to help focus your attention. They are somewhat lengthy, but they are meant to alert you in to all the potentially meaningful details, not just the obvious ones. Although the forms are straightforward, we will explain some of the crucial aspects of a thorough Accident Report because it is more important for you to understand the types of things to note at the scene than to mechanistically follow the forms.

ACCIDENT REPORT INFORMATION

Witnesses.

- Don't expect everyone involved in an accident to agree on how or why it happened. Sometimes, when people realize the potential economic trauma resulting from the accident, recollections of the accident change into self-serving testimonials. In a time of a crisis it can be hard to believe that **you** made a stupid driving error that resulted in a crash. To make matters more confusing, police reports might contain only the conflicting statements of those involved in the accident. As a result, insurance companies put a big emphasis on the statements of impartial witnesses. The statement of a reliable witness can quickly resolve an otherwise difficult situation.

- Try to get the name, address, and phone number of any possible witness. People are often hesitant to give out personal information. If so, offer your business card or even give out the name of your insurance company and policy number so the person can contact your insurer directly. If they won't talk to you, encourage witnesses to offer their statements or at least their names to the police.

- Finally, don't get caught up trying to convince a reluctant witness to cooperate. Move on to find someone else. Witnesses are likely to disappear from the scene quickly once the action settles down. If you feel that a reluctant person might be important, get his or her auto make, model, and license number if possible. Your insurer can follow up with this information during its investigation.

Physical setting of accident.

- As accurately and in as much detail as possible, note the physical setting of the accident. Draw an accident diagram showing streets, the location of traffic signals, vehicle direction/motion, pedestrian traffic, skid marks (pace out and estimate their length), and any other illustrative details.

- Also note any limitations on visibility, the condition of traffic control signals, the condition of the roadway, and weather and lighting conditions. Consider the accident from the other driver's perspective. Were there physical objects that obscured the view or in some way contributed to the accident?

- Note the time of the accident. It can help determine weather, lighting, road conditions, traffic congestion, and many other relevant factors.

Vehicle inspection.

- Inspect all the vehicles involved, noting the damage (if you can, differentiate between pre-existing damage and that caused by the accident) and the general condition of each. Note burned out head lamps or taillights, or other obvious defects. Expired registration or safety inspection stickers might indicate mechanical problems with the vehicle. If there are open alcoholic beverage containers in the vehicle let the police know immediately.

Other driver(s).

- Obviously, you need a good deal of information from the other driver(s) involved. You need a name, address, phone number, driver's license number, vehicle make, model, and tag number, and the name, policy number, and phone number of the insurer for each driver.

- Note if a person's driver's license requires the use of corrective lenses and whether he or she is wearing them. Jot down any other apparent conditions, such as physical disabilities, the smell of liquor, slurred speech, or verbal remarks about the cause of the accident.

Safety Equipment.

- As best you can, determine whether safety belts were being used by everyone involved in the accident. In some jurisdictions, if you are injured in an accident and were not wearing a seat belt, you are considered partly at fault and can lose all right to a damage claim.
- Look and see if seat belts are missing, pushed down behind the seat back, or lying buckled on the seat (to trick the warning buzzer). Have the police verify your findings if possible.

Passengers.

- If you can, get the names, addresses, etc. of passengers in the other vehicles, especially those who are injured. This information isn't vital; most likely, the information will be accessible if they later make a claim against your insurer or the driver of their vehicle. If you can, record where in the vehicle each passenger was sitting.

Injuries.

- As you get information from other drivers and passengers, note any apparent injuries or other details you think might be important. Often, if a passenger has been drinking, the driver has as well.

Describe the Accident.

- Round out the report with a narrative of what happened, including why the accident happened, what steps you took to avoid it, and what you think the other driver could have done differently. Elaborate on any details you think are important and not covered elsewhere in the report.

Photographs.

- If someone has a camera available, take pictures. A photograph of missing seat belts or minor vehicle damage later claimed (or made to be) major could save you or your insurer thousands of dollars and hours of frustration. If the accident involves a number of vehicles or took place at an unusual location take as many pictures as necessary to capture all the damage and the complexity of the situation.

Police report.

- Jot down the names and badge numbers of the police who are at the scene and make sure you know how to get a copy of the police report. It usually takes a day or two of processing before it is available.

TALK ABOUT THE ACCIDENT TO THE POLICE ONLY

Most lawyers will recommend that you bite your tongue and fight your inclination to discuss the accident with anyone at the scene except the police. The problem, they say, is that your apologies, admissions, and even off-hand statements like being at an office party before the accident, could come back to haunt you as a legal matter. Also, for accidents of any significance, there will be all sorts of bystanders, some of whom may be attorneys (or their runners) or passengers (who are probably friends of the other driver) from the other vehicle(s). Unfortunately, the friendly face you confide in could end up legally representing the other driver or testifying on his or her behalf. Without knowing all the circumstances, you may talk about how you think you caused the accident when, in fact, you were not entirely to blame.

Steve

> *I was driving through a wooded residential area. In the twilight the street signs were difficult to find, let alone read. I was fumbling with a handwritten map, trying to figure out which direction to go. At one intersection, I looked up from my map and at first glance didn't see the red traffic signal. I looked to the corners of the intersection, trying to find a familiar street name and then casually looked up the roadway again. This time I saw the red light, but couldn't stop in time. Skidding into the intersection, my car was plowed into from the side.*

> *I ran out of my car to check on the other driver and immediately began apologizing profusely. Over and over, to anyone who would listen, I told how I didn't see the light until it was too late and how thankful I was that no one was hurt.*

> *Luckily, there were witnesses who saw the accident from both sides of the intersection. It turned out that the light signal had malfunctioned, and in fact, the light was red from both sides of the intersection. The other driver, who was too shaken to speak, had run the red light as well.*

Fault and liability are legal questions to be addressed after all the facts pertaining to the accident have been examined. In most situations you should give your statement to the police only. And when you do, just describe the accident—as they said on Dragnet, "just the facts ma'am"—and otherwise control your words until you've assessed the entire situation.

At the same time, we are not suggesting that you withhold facts. You must honestly acknowledge your actions as they relate to the accident. And once the facts are clear, an honest, sincere apology can be an expression of your integrity as well as a component of your own healing and that of the other party.

DON'T MAKE DEALS AT THE SCENE

You can wait until you get away from the accident scene and have some time to calm down before contacting your insurer. Ninety-nine per cent of the time there is no reason to make a quick cash deal with the other driver. If the other driver is clearly at fault, admits it, and offers a few hundred dollars to resolve the situation, we suggest you do everything listed in the above sections and politely ask that you be given a day or two to consider the offer. You need to give your body and your common sense some time to relax and take inventory. If you leave with $200 dollars in your pocket and no information about the other driver, or even worse, no names of witnesses, you may be paying for your own medical treatment when your back starts to stiffen or your neck starts to hurt. Take your time, and if a day or two later you are feeling fine, you can then decide whether a couple of hundred dollars is reasonable compensation. If the other driver really wants to keep his/her insurer out of the picture, the offer should still be available. If not, you have all the information you need to make an insurance claim.

If you are at fault and want to settle the claim at the scene, the cash you give away will not necessarily stop the other person from making a claim against your insurance policy. The only way to bar future claims relating to the accident is to obtain an enforceable "release from liability" agreement. A verbal agreement to forego future claims in exchange for a small amount of cash, made in the heat of the moment after the accident, is probably not enforceable in court, especially if the person later proves to be seriously injured.

On the other hand, if in a day or two the other driver is willing to sign a release in exchange for your cash offer and you have decided to handle the situation without your insurance company, the agreement should protect you.

It may take a few days for you to be fully aware of the physical and emotional impact of an accident. It is a smart, self-protective decision to give yourself time to consider the consequences of any private settlement you might get involved with.

Do not make a deal with an attorney who may show up at the accident scene. If someone wants to give you a business card, accept it, but put some time and distance between you and the physical setting of the accident drama before accepting any legal representation.

You must use your own judgment; just be careful and discriminating.

FOLLOW UP MEDICAL TREATMENT

Once you have obtained all the information you need, and if necessary, arranged for your vehicle to be towed, you are ready to leave the accident scene. Even if you feel fine, if you were bounced around by the force of the accident, consider going to see your physician or a chiropractor for an examination. Traumatic Brain Injury can occur when the brain bangs up against the skull. You don't have to hit your head or be knocked unconscious to experience a force hard enough to cause a closed head injury. If the accident damaged ligaments or tendons, pinched a nerve or a spinal disc, or caused a slight misalignment of your spine, the disabling symptoms may not be apparent for a day or two. Often the pain comes a few days after the accident when the muscles and supporting structure around the injury begin to strain from overcompensating for the injured area.

Just because you do not feel pain, does not mean the injury is not present. An experienced accident injury specialist can diagnosis most injuries immediately using finger pressure and limited range of motion tests, called motion palpation. If an injury is diagnosed before there is significant swelling and motion impairment, you can often avoid a good deal of pain. When identified early you are less likely to inadvertently aggravate an injury. Certainly, the sooner an aggressive treatment and rehabilitation program is started, the quicker and more efficiently your injuries heal.

FIND QUIET TIME FOR YOURSELF

Once you are safely away from the accident scene, it is time to acknowledge the emotional force of the incident. Within a day or two after the accident, find some quiet time to relieve the tension from your body. If you can, take a day off from work and let the healing magic of sleep do its work. It is also healing to talk about the experience. Whether it is with a friend, a spouse, or a medical professional, talk through your emotional experience of the accident and let go of the trauma through your tears and your voice. Regardless of how minor the wreck may appear in retrospect, believing, even for a moment, that you, or someone in your car was going to be killed or injured, can be a life-altering event. However you do it, be kind to yourself by acknowledging the added emotional weight the accident has forced onto your shoulders.

THE ACCIDENT EXPERIENCE LOG

You should begin an "Accident Experience Log" immediately following the wreck. In this log, you should document everything related to the accident. For example, all the information you have collected at the scene should be kept in this log. You should also keep a continuous diary of phone calls, correspondence, and bills relating to your recovery. In addition, you should keep a running diary of your physical and emotional treatment and healing.

There are a number of reasons this log is important. First, an ongoing record is a much more reliable and accurate method of documenting your case than a rough reconstruction months after the accident. The better you can document your claims, the more apt you will be to get the settlement you deserve. Not only are tangible medical bills important, an honest ongoing account of your emotional and physical healing process is useful in evaluating your economic recovery as well.

If a criminal case is involved such as in drunk driving, such a log can be useful when asked to write a Victim Impact Statement. Keep in mind that the log may be considered "discoverable" in a criminal or civil case and a copy turned over to the other side.

Recording your ongoing healing process, how you feel and what treatment you have received, will help you communicate with the medical professionals treating you. In addition it will give you some perspective on your own progress. It can be comforting to be able to review your progress from week to week.

The log itself need not be fancy. A three-ring notebook or an expandable accordion file will work best. Any system where you can keep an ongoing written journal/log and keep loose bills and letters together is what you need.

CONCLUSION

The major points to remember in helping yourself at the accident scene are:

- Keep control of your emotions at the scene, especially your anger.
- Safety is the first priority. Make sure appropriate medical and safety professionals are notified and ongoing accident danger is minimized.
- Complete your own accident report in addition to the official police report.

- Observe all the details; an unused seat belt, an expired safety inspection, an obstructed traffic signal. You never know what might make the critical difference in your economic recovery.

- Control your tongue and only discuss circumstances of the accident with the police. There will be time and opportunity for apologies later.

- Be very careful making deals with other drivers at the accident scene. There is no reason to hurry; you will be in a much more realistic emotional state after giving yourself a day or two to calm down and allowing your body time to stabilize.

- Do not hesitate to get medical attention.

- Once away from the accident scene, find time to get rid of the stress of the experience. Allow yourself to ventilate, cry, and talk about what happened.

NOTES

Chapter 3

ACCIDENT INJURIES

HOW ACCIDENTS INJURE YOUR BODY

The combinations of physical injuries you might suffer as a result of a car accident can vary tremendously. What is common to all your injuries is pain.

Roy

I was the maintenance supervisor for a large chemical manufacturer. I was responsible for a number of facilities spread over several miles in the rural part of the country. Most days I probably criss-crossed over 100 miles in my pickup, fixing a ruptured pipe here, a broken pump there. My truck-bed was always loaded with metal pipes, tools, and small machinery.

On one of my trips, I swerved to avoid a deer in the road. I lost control of the truck and slammed into a utility pole. Luckily, I was wearing a seat belt so I wasn't thrown through the windshield — that's how hard I hit the pole. But one small diameter pipe lying loose in the flatbed was launched forward

*through my rear window. The pipe speared through
my shoulder muscles. The fire department rescue
team had to cut off the three foot tail-end of the pipe
sticking out the rear window to free me from my
truck.*

As an accident victim, you are faced with a trauma you
never expected. You know you hurt, sometimes to a degree you could not imagine. The one thing you know for
sure, you want your physical pain to go away, as quickly as
possible.

The cause of Roy's pain is fairly obvious. As a reminder
of how good it feels to be pain free, Roy carries a key ring
made from a small length of pipe removed from his shoulder. But how do you determine the cause of your pain if
the injury is not so apparent? Your lower back may hurt,
badly. Did the accident damage the bones of the spinal
column, or the supporting muscles, tendons, and ligaments? Before you can make the proper choices in getting
the best, most comprehensive treatment, you should have
an understanding of the parts of the body most commonly
injured in car accidents. With this knowledge as a basis,
you can be more intelligently involved in choosing treatment appropriate to healing your injuries.

BONES

Your bones, all 206 of them, give your body its basic
structure and shape. They lie within the soft tissues of the
body and are dynamic, living structures capable of growth
and regeneration.

The sudden, pounding impact of a car accident can
cause three types of bone injuries: fractures, compound
fractures, and bruises. The most common fracture is either
a "break," which is a complete severing of the bone or a
"greenstick" fracture, which is a cracking of the bone.

Janice

My husband was driving us down a mountain road one evening after a long day of skiing. He was tired and anxious to get home, probably going too fast for the road conditions. He lost control going around a curve and the car spun off the edge of the road. As we rolled down the short embankment, my right arm whipped against the doorframe sharply, snapping one of the bones in my forearm. I could see the broken edge of the bone bulging against my skin. My shoulder also pounded into the door over and over as we rolled. The tip of my shoulder was swollen and tender for several weeks.

When the fractured bone lacerates the surrounding soft tissue, like Janice's forearm protruding through her skin, the injury is called a compound fracture. This type of injury is generally more severe and much more painful than a simple fracture.

Bone fractures usually heal well. The fracture heals as though a coating of super-glue was added around the bone. In some cases the healed bone may be stronger than it was before the injury. Fractures may take between two and twelve months to heal, depending upon which bone is fractured, the location of the fracture on the bone, and the severity of the break. Surgery may be required for the proper treatment of some fractures.

It is important to get fractures treated quickly and properly. If a fracture is not properly treated, the bone might heal abnormally and create chronic musculature problems. In some cases, if a bone heals incorrectly, it must be surgically rebroken and reset.

Bone bruises can be just as painful, although usually not as debilitating as fractures. Like our bodies, bones have a vascular skinlike covering. The covering also holds a small amount of fluid that bathes and nourishes the bone within. Bones can be bruised by banging into something, like Janice's shoulder pounding into the door frame. The bruised bone is accompanied by a swelling of the bone covering. The swelling is really extra fluid that helps protect and heal the bruised bone. Bruised bones usually heal more quickly than fractures, with little potential for long-term complications.

SOFT TISSUE

There are a variety of specialized tissue types making up the human body. The term "soft tissue" is really a descriptive classification which includes the many different types of tissue that are soft to the touch. Muscles, cartilage, tendons, ligaments, scar tissue, and skin are the soft tissue types most commonly injured in an automobile accident.

Sara

Sarah was only going about 20 mph when the car in the oncoming lane drifted across the divider. She and the other driver were busy watching all the Sunday beach activity on the sides of the road. By the time she glanced ahead the other car was almost on top of her.

She slammed down the brake pedal, locking her right knee. Out of habit, she had moved the shoulder strap of her seat belt behind her back because it irritated her neck and chin. On impact her torso flung forward against the steering wheel. Luckily the waist strap kept her bottom on the seat, preventing her head from smashing through the windshield.

Nevertheless, the force of the upper half of her body being thrown toward the windshield and then abruptly stopped by the belt across her hips put a tremendous stress on her lower back. The support-ing structure of her lower back was severely strained.

Her forward motion was stopped by the steering wheel. First her mouth crunched against the hard plastic wheel, puncturing lower and upper lip and snapping her head back. The upper half of her torso also struck the wheel. The curve of the steering wheel left a bruise across her chest.

Sarah was able to pull herself out of the car, but she looked and felt like she had gone 15 rounds with Mohammed Ali. Blood was seeping from her punc-tured lip and her face stung. She had trouble stand-ing because the muscles in her lower back were in spasm. Whenever she put weight on her right brak-ing leg, the under side of her knee screamed in pain. Her neck was stiff and she had a hurricane force headache behind her temples. Even the slight ten-sion of her bra hurt her chest.

Astonishingly enough, the puncture in Sarah's lip was her only visible injury. If you were to look at Sarah follow-ing her accident you would not see her internal trauma. Her cuts and facial bruises healed quickly. Once they healed the only physical reminder of the accident would be her internal pain. Although the pain from soft tissue injuries is real, the tendency is to discount the existence of these injuries because they are so difficult to diagnose precisely, and therefore, to treat effectively.

As an accident victim with soft tissue injuries you might feel like a child complaining of phantom stomach aches on the first day of school. It is hard to take your injuries seriously; after all, from the outside you look fine. So you might try to ignore your injuries and your pain as best you can. You might even begin to doubt the "reality" of your pain and feel embarrassed about seeking medical attention.

Be assured, soft tissue injuries are as real and substantial, as the accompanying pain. In fact, soft tissue damage is the most common type of accident injury and is also the most misunderstood, misdiagnosed, and mistreated. Unfortunately and unnecessarily, the mistakes made in treating soft tissue injury may result in chronic pain and lifelong disabilities.

Part of the difficulty in proper diagnosis and treatment is the variety of soft tissue types and the complex interrelationships between these tissues. Even with a detailed knowledge of human anatomy, it can be hard to determine whether Sarah's lower back pain is due to damaged tendons, ligaments, or muscles. They are attached to each other and function as one unit. But complexity doesn't mean proper diagnosis and treatment is impossible. It just requires a systematic, conscientious approach by a medical professional and an informed, diligent, and involved patient.

DO NOT fall into the denial trap. If your body is in pain, do not ignore it. There are effective treatment methodologies available to treat the majority of soft tissue injuries. You do not have to live with your pain. In fact, the more you ignore your body's dysfunction the more likely your injury will become chronically painful and debilitating. It is **your** body that hurts, and it is the only one **you** have.

MUSCLES

Muscles move the body. The only actions they can perform are contracting and shortening, relaxing and lengthening. A muscle is made up of thousands of separate fibers. The fibers contract and relax as a group causing movement.

Muscle tissue is filled with thousands of blood vessels giving it its "steak" red color. The blood vessels supply the tissue with oxygen and nutrients and carry away the waste products created by muscle movement. Normally, muscle tissue heals very quickly because so much nourishing blood circulates within it. Muscle healing time is related to the severity of the injury, but most injuries heal within a few weeks.

An automobile accident can cause three types of muscle damage: strained muscle, torn muscle fibers, and bruised muscle tissue. Muscles get strained by excessive stress or overuse. Sore shoulders, arms, and thighs are all common post-accident symptoms, probably resulting from bracing yourself for impact by tensing the large muscle in your body. Muscle strain is accompanied by mild swelling and pain over a wide area which disappears in a few days.

A more serious muscle injury occurs when muscle fiber tears. The severity of this type of injury varies greatly. When a small number of fibers tear, the healing may only take a week or two. If more fibers are torn, the injury will be more severe, causing greater pain and a more lengthy healing process.

For example, the spasm in Sarah's lower back could be the result of strained or torn muscle tissue. There are about 2,000 muscles in the back and neck that control movement. Muscle spasm is a protective, involuntary contraction your body uses to prevent movement in an injured area. Therefore, muscle spasm is usually the result of an injury and not an injury in itself. It is associated with many kinds of injuries like torn ligaments and tendons, irritated joints, pinched nerves, and damaged muscle tissue.

The third type of injury is a muscle bruise or hematoma. This results from a blow severe enough to break blood vessels within the muscle tissue. Sarah's soreness is a result of bruised muscle and skin tissue. The impact of her chest against the steering wheel broke blood vessels and caused blood to seep out into a broad area. The result is swelling, discoloration, and discomfort. Healing time depends upon the severity of the bruise.

TENDONS

Tendons are the connecting link between muscles and bones. They are made up of a tough, white, fibrous material. Normally, tendons do not stretch or contract like muscles. Tendons have very little blood supply and therefore can take a very long time to heal from an injury.

Unfortunately, the sudden, jolting impact of an automobile accident quite commonly causes tendon injuries. A tendon can be injured in one of three places: it can tear away slightly from where it is attached to the bone (this is very common), some of the fibers in the main body of the tendon can tear, or the tendon might tear away from where it attaches to the muscle.

Usually when a tendon is injured, only some of the fibers tear; tendons rarely rip completely in half. The higher the proportion of fibers damaged, the more severe the injury. Of course, more severe injuries are more painful and require a longer healing time.

It can be difficult to determine whether it is the tendon that has been injured or just the associated muscle, since they function as one unit. As we mentioned, the muscles surrounding a damaged tendon often go into spasm as a protective function. While tendons are healing, or when healing is incomplete, they remain vulnerable to reinjury because the tendon is structurally weak. For example, the pain in Sarah's knee resulted from reinjury of her weak hamstring tendon (it connects the large hamstring muscle of the thigh to the knee area). She had injured the tendons playing football with her brothers as a young girl. When she "straight-legged" her brake pedal, the stress manifested in the weakest area of her leg, the tendons of her knee.

An injured tendon may heal poorly (with a lot of scar tissue) if it is repeatedly re-strained. If tendon injuries do not receive proper treatment, they can take months or even years to heal.

LIGAMENTS

Ligaments, like tendons, are made up of a tough, white, fibrous material. They also have very limited blood supply and thus heal very slowly. The function of ligaments is quite different from tendons. Ligaments hold bones together at the joints and limit their range of motion. For example, several ligaments hold your upper arm to your shoulder; other ligaments hold your vertebrae into the semi-flexible structure of the spine.

Ligaments, like tendons, are not very elastic and thus do not stretch. Ligaments can be damaged when they are fatigued or are abnormally stressed. The sudden, violent impact of an automobile collision can over-extend joints which may cause ligament injury. For example, the strain Sarah experienced on her lower back probably damaged ligaments. It doesn't take much stress to cause damage to the lower back, as those with chronic back trouble know.

When a ligament is injured, it can tear partially or completely. Commonly, some of the ligament fibers tear slightly, like the fraying of a rope. When ligaments are damaged, the joint they support becomes weak and unstable. When even a slight tear occurs, the area can become inflamed and movement becomes quite painful. Once again, muscle spasm almost always accompany damaged ligaments.

Sometimes, as the fibers of the ligament begin to heal, they adhere to the adjacent bone, attaching to an abnormal area on the bone with scar tissue. This is called adhesion. This can severely limit the free movement of the bone. Often, the fibers in this area re-tear as they are exercised and pulled away from the area of the bone they are adhered to. The area may become inflamed and painful as the ligaments once again heal. The repeated cycle of adhering and tearing is what causes some ligament injuries to become chronically debilitating.

SPINAL DISCS

The vertebrae in your spine are cushioned and separated from one another by intervertebral discs. The discs are semi-flexible, compressible structures made of two different types of cartilage. Spinal discs have almost no blood supply, so when damaged they heal very slowly.

When the sudden jolting impact of a car accident crushes or cracks the shock-absorbing cartilage in the spine, the pain is not actually from the disc itself. The disc has few associated nerves. Rather, it is the displaced cartilage that is pressing on an adjacent nerve and/or causing abnormal tension on the supporting soft tissues that causes pain.

Thus, when Sarah's head thrust forward and then was snapped back abruptly by the steering wheel she may have damaged an intervertebral disc in her neck. The oncoming ache in her temples could result from a pinched nerve. The general tension in her neck could be due to the abnormal strain on the supporting tissue.

It is important to note that the symptoms and pain caused by intervertebral disc problems can be mimicked by damaged tendons or ligaments. Correctly determining the actual damage can be difficult.

SCAR TISSUE

Normally, the fibers of tendons, muscles, or ligaments run parallel to one another, somewhat like the rows and rows of corn in Iowa. Torn fibers disrupt the uniformity of the tissue, like a road cut across a field of corn. Ideally, the fibers should heal back into parallel rows, like replanting the rows over the road cut. Unfortunately, sometimes this does not happen. Rather than rejoining across the tear, end-to-end, adjacent fibers sometimes join together, side-by-side. It is as if someone randomly planted the corn over and around the road cut, ignoring the parallel rows. The healing area becomes a disorganized mass of tissue. If the area is re-stressed, the fibers can re-tear and the pain and inflammation is aggravated. Once again, as the fibers heal, they stick together in all directions. The final result is the formation of weak and sometimes painful scar tissue.

This abnormal tissue forms a weak area subject to recurring muscle, tendon, or ligament injuries. The sudden bangs and jolts of a car accident wreak havoc on previously weakened areas of the body. Often, as a result of accidents, trick knees do their tricks, bad backs flare up, and tennis elbows will not play anymore. Remember, scar tissue forms as a result of improper healing. Often with proper care, these sensitive areas can heal correctly.

SKIN

The skin is one of the most important organs of the body. The skin is a complex organ made up of nerves, hair follicles, oil glands, blood vessels, fat cells, and more. It is a tough conglomerate of tissue; its main functions are perception of, and protection from, changes in the external environment.

Car accidents can cause open and closed skin wounds. When the skin tissue is damaged without a break in the surface of the skin, the wound is closed. If the skin is broken, it is an open wound. A closed skin wound, called a bruise or contusion, is usually caused by striking a blunt object. The skin tissue is crushed, and varying amounts of blood and cellular fluid leak into the surrounding tissue. If the blow is severe enough, the tissue beneath the skin may be damaged as well.

Open wounds cause obvious bleeding and are subject to further complications due to infection.

Tim

I saw the other car barreling through the red light when I was halfway across the intersection. It was too late for me to do anything but brace himself for the impact. The other car struck me squarely on the driver's side. My head snapped sideways into the collapsing door and bounced off the edge of my open window. The window-lip split the skin across my temple and the edge of my forehead. It took forty-five stitches to close the gash.

Tim knew what he needed and where to go to treat his open skin wound. It was obvious that his wound needed stitching up. He could go to a hospital emergency room or possibly his family physician and get the proper treatment. Skin tissue is replete with blood vessels and thus skin wounds need little ongoing therapy to heal properly. A wound like Tim's heals relatively quickly if kept clean and protected. The time it takes for this type of wound to heal is more dependent on diet and lifestyle than on any continuing medical therapy.

This is not the case for some of the other soft tissue injuries discussed in this chapter. Sarah's knee, back, and neck injuries described above, for example, require an ongoing and evolving treatment methodology for proper healing.

CONCLUSION

Luckily, medical understanding of the healing process has come a long way since the days of miracle elixirs. As discussed in the next chapter, there are a wide variety of effective treatment methodologies available to heal your injuries.

Chapter 4

HEALING YOUR BODY

IT IS YOUR BODY THAT HURTS

Your body doesn't lie. Whether sick or healthy, like a precocious child it continually tells its story. After an accident your back may ache, your neck may be stiff, you might even have trouble sleeping. All these symptoms are your body's way of communicating, its way of telling a story about its state of health or disease. The challenge is learning to listen to, and **really** hear, its messages.

Being attentive to your body's messages can be difficult, but pain's signals are the keys to your healing process. Listening to your body and making the right choices for healing is a very personal process. After all, it is **your** body; only **you** know when it feels right and healthy and when it doesn't.

YOU ARE RESPONSIBLE FOR YOUR BODY

The extent of your responsiblity in the healing process is much more than getting your body to the family doctor and hanging on for the ride. While this passive approach works in some situations, with many accident injuries it is likely to leave you frustrated and in pain for an extended period.

One of the reasons for this is because knowledge about healing the body is ever-changing; new treatments are constantly evolving. Some medical practitioners and most injured people do not arealize the full range of medical treatment available. Medical professionals can become too myopic with their own specialities and lose sight of alternatives. Until now you probably knew very little about your body and even less about the healing process.

In fact, most accident injuries require a multifaceted treatment approach to heal properly and efficiently. For example, proper treatment of strained neck ligaments or tendons should involve massage, chiropractic manipulation, exercise, and physical therapy, at a minimum! If you used a passive approach in healing this injury you would probably end up using pain killers (usually addictive narcotics), wearing a neck brace, and complaining for months about how badly you feel. Even if the pain eventually went away using this approach, you would never regain full neck strength and freedom of movement. Unless the medical practitioner upon whom you depend is well informed and understands the benefits of a multifaceted treatment approach, you stand the chance of getting improper or inefficient treatment.

You can't really change the treatment style of any of the medical professionals you see, but you can make responsible choices about whom you pay for treatment. Armed with the information in this chapter, you can be an active participant in your healing process and find your way to health quickly. And remember, only **you** really know **your** body, when it feels right and when it doesn't.

CHOOSING YOUR PRIMARY CAREGIVER

Ideally, the process of healing complex injuries should play like the London Philharmonic Symphony. Your injuries dictate the type of medical music to be played; the tempo and mix of the medical musicians working with you should evolve as the needs of your healing body change. And most important, the work of the conductor should be performed by two, you and a primary caregiver.

Choosing the person you rely upon to help guide your healing process, your co-conductor or primary caregiver, is crucial. You probably would not expect your family physician to perform a complex knee surgery. Rather, you would look to a specialist. Accident injuries, especially extensive soft tissue damage, can be equally complicated and usually requires an elaborate treatment methodology. To receive the best advice and to participate in a favorable healing process you need someone skilled in this area of medicine. Although they are rare, we recommend that you find a physician who specializes in the treatment of accident injuries. This type of professional should be well versed in the various treatment methodologies effective with accident injuries and will understand the evolutionary nature of their healing process.

If you are not able to find this type of specialist, then a Sports Medicine specialist or clinic, orthopedist, chiropractor, osteopath, or physical therapist might fit the bill. The most important point is to be assertive in asking questions and communicating with whomever you invite to participate in your healing process. You might use the phone to interview a few practitioners about their specialities and treatment preferences. Attorneys who specialize in personal injury work are also very good sources because they use physicians as expert witnesses. Finally, ask your friends or co-workers whom they've had experience with. You will be surprised at how many people have been injured in an accident. Find out who and what helped them. If you do not feel you are getting the attention you need, go elsewhere.

As mentioned above, your injuries dictate the treatment needed. Ideally, your physician will have a detailed understanding of your injuries and the progression of treatments they require. Your physician/co-conductor monitors your progress and adjusts the emphasis of the other medical musicians assisting in your treatment.

As your body heals, a variety of medical professionals will take part in the treatment process. There could be a chiropractor, a masseuse, a physical therapist, and possibly a psychotherapist involved in your healing process. Each of these medical professionals needs to be aware of the state of your body, how your healing has progressed, and the various types of treatments you are participating in. They rely on you to keep them informed.

One of the tools you can use to help you keep the medical practitioners informed is the Accident Logbook discussed in Chapter 2. A portion of the log should be dedicated to documenting your physical healing process.

DESCRIPTION OF ACCIDENT

First, you should write a description of the accident itself with an emphasis on describing how your body was injured. Include the direction of impact, speed, how your body moved, where you ended up after the impact, and how your pain developed. Injury diagnosis, particularly soft tissue damage assessment, can depend upon this type of information. For example, a head-on collision might damage a different area of your neck than a side impact would. All you might feel is general pain and stiffness, but the damaged area, and thus the treatment might vary.

Document everything related to your physical healing; where you feel pain, in what way your movement is abnormally limited, the types of treatment you are involved with, and generally how you perceive your healing. This requires some discipline on your part. You should make entries daily, even if you do not have much to say other than that there has been no change from the previous day.

Pay particular attention to your entries on the days when you receive treatment. Review your log before your appointment to use it as a communication tool. For example, it helps the physical therapist to know that when the chiropractor adjusted your lower back, the tension in your leg subsided. Knowing this, the physical therapist might adjust your routine to help strengthen your lower back muscles. Your memory might be good, but you will not forget to communicate an important detail when it is written down. Also document your progress; looking back over a few weeks and seeing your own progress is healing in itself.

Hopefully, your co-conductor is actively playing his/her part in the communication process as well. Ideally, the primary caregiver is communicating with the other medical professionals directly. In the same way that you give a status update on each visit, your co-conductor should be communicating his/her own impressions and recommendations to the other therapists.

Even if your co-conductor or primary caregiver is not communicating directly with the other medical professionals, then he/she should be co-conducting through you. The primary caregiver can do this by monitoring your healing process both through physical examinations and by utilizing the information you communicate. He/she can recommend adjustments in the types of treatments you receive, their frequency, and from whom you receive treatment.

Regardless of who you choose to be your primary treatment advisor, whether it is an accident injury specialist, a chiropractor, a physical therapist, or your family physician, the goal of your treatment program should be to heal your body to the greatest possible degree in the shortest possible time. Ideally, this means that rehabilitation should begin at the same time as injury treatment. Treatment and rehabilitation should blend imperceptibly into one, minimizing the effects of the injury. When rehabilitation is started while healing is taking place, the quality of the tissue that forms during the healing process is improved. The aim is not necessarily to speed up healing—your body sets its own pace—but to do all that is possible to avoid slowing it down.

TREATMENT METHODOLOGIES

The following is a fairly comprehensive description of treatments which can be successfully used to help heal accident injuries. The most successful treatment course utilizes a number of treatment methodologies and changes as injuries heal. You are encouraged to maintain an open, inquisitive, and careful approach to your healing process. Medical knowledge and treatment is not static. No one specialty has a corner on the treatment market. The following discussion covers some relatively unconventional medical approaches as well as traditional ones. They all have merit when used appropriately.

MEDICATION AND REST

Accident victims frequently leave their doctor's office with a prescription for some type of oral medication and the advice to rest.

Lester

Lester was rear-ended by a utility truck while stopped at an intersection. Lester was an exceptionally tall man, but he hadn't adjusted his headrest to properly support his head. Instead, the headrest acted as a fulcrum when his head whipped backward on impact. The supporting ligaments in his neck were severely strained.

As often happens with these types of soft tissue injuries, Lester was able to walk away from the accident feeling only slight discomfort in his neck. The well developed muscles in his neck overcompensated for the strained ligaments.

It wasn't until the middle of the night that his neck muscles started to spasm. He figured the discomfort would go away with a couple of aspirin. By morning he could barely lift his head off the pillow without bolts of pain shooting out from his neck and shoulders. Once he got to his feet , he couldn't turn his neck from side to side without feeling like someone was hammering nails into his spine.

Amazingly enough, Lester decided he could live with the discomfort; he assumed the tension would go away within a couple of days. He didn't connect the specific events of the accident, the abnormal and excessive whipping of his neck, to his pain. He gobbled a few aspirins and went off to work. By evening his whole head was pounding. The pain was persistent even when he wasn't trying to swivel his head. It felt like his neck was in a vise. He had about 2 hours of fitful sleep that night.

Lester was a healthy, strong man. The last time he saw his doctor was when his wife gave birth to their 15 year-old daughter. He was stubborn, but his neck was screaming for something. When he finally went to see the doctor he was immediately put in a neck brace. The doctor told Lester he needed to rest his neck and gave him a prescription for Valium to help relax his tense muscles. Lester dutifully took his drugs and as much as his work allowed, rested his neck. He never imagined there was anything more he might do to facilitate his healing.

Lester wore the neck brace on and off for six months. On bad days he still needed the Valium to reduce his neck tension and pain. To this day, he still gets unexplained headaches and neckaches. He also feels like he has lost a lot of the strength in his neck. If he turns his neck too quickly or abruptly his muscles still have a tendency to spasm and complain with pain.

Medication and rest alone are the most common, and the least effective, combination of therapies modern medicine has to offer. Rest, as a form of medical therapy, is cheap and easy. Given time and patience, rest works for mild injuries such as slight muscle strains or inflammation. Certainly, getting plenty of sleep is vital to the healing process. But most significant injuries never heal properly when the only structured form of treatment utilized is rest. For example, regardless of the amount of time given for rest to work, it is an ineffective treatment for torn ligaments and tendons.

Rest alone promotes the formation of painful scar tissue and adhesions. Taking excessive stress off the injured area through rest helps the healing process by allowing the body some time to repair the tissue. But along with rest, it is important to move the injured body part without stressing it. This helps prevent the formation of scar tissue and adhesions, promotes blood circulation, and reduces muscle degeneration or atrophy. When muscle tissue isn't used it breaks down; this process is called muscle atrophy. Disuse of muscles and tendons also causes other cellular changes which weaken the tissue further. Overall, rest unnecessarily weakens tissue structure making it especially vulnerable to re-injury. Lester's damaged neck ligaments would heal properly with an aggressive treatment program aimed at rehabilitating the damaged area in a controlled manner.

Medication is effective in a limited way. It is normally taken to relieve pain and/or to reduce inflammation. But medication generally does not aid the healing process. Short term pain relief can be important, especially the first few days after the accident, but true pain relief will only come with proper healing of damaged tissue.

Oral medication can be helpful when used in conjunction with a rehabilitation program. Medication can help reduce swelling and take the edge off painful injuries, which allows for increased mobility of the affected area. With some reduction of pain, an active rehabilitation can begin shortly after the injury occurs. Anti-inflammatory agents, analgesics, and muscle relaxants are the three most common types of medication prescribed.

Anti-inflammatory drugs, such as Cortisone (steroidal) and Motrin (non-steroidal), are used to reduce the swelling that accompanies some injuries. Swelling is a painful symptom of damaged tissue. Reducing the swelling with drugs offers some temporary pain relief while healing progresses.

Analgesics such as Codeine and Darvon, or stronger varieties like Demerol and Percodan, are very effective painkillers. They numb your mind to the pain in your body, but they have no healing effect whatsoever. Obviously, for serious injuries the pain relief analgesics provide can be a God-send.

Muscle relaxants such as Valium and Robaxin temporarily reduce muscle tension. Like most other forms of oral medication, their main function is to reduce pain and discomfort. It is important not to confuse true health with the pain-free mask drugs provide. Pain is a symptom of damaged tissue, masking the symptom is not a sign of healed tissue.

In some cases, initially, any form of pain relief is a priority. But once the pain of damaged tissue is manageable, the focus should shift to healing damaged tissue, not just masking its symptoms. Also, most medications have some side effects, particularly if they are taken for an extended period of time. They may effect your digestion, alertness, blood pressure, and emotional state. They may also be addictive.

PHYSICAL THERAPY

Physical therapy techniques can be the cornerstone of an effective rehabilitation program. Physical therapy uses heat (in the form of microwave, ultrasound, whirlpools, light, and hot packs), ice therapy, manual or electronic massage, and controlled movement and exercise for injury treatment and rehabilitation. Physical therapy promotes blood circulation in injured areas through the use of heat, cold, and controlled movement. Also, a well designed movement and exercise regime in physical therapy limits the production of scar tissue and adhesions and promotes the formation of healthy pliable tissue. Finally, physical therapy helps maintain muscle strength and flexibility while healing is taking place.

Physical therapists use heat in the form of warm baths, hot packs, and heat lamps to treat some injuries. Just about every household in America owns a heating pad and before electricity people used hot compresses to treat painful injuries. Heat increases blood circulation in the skin, muscles, tendons, and ligaments that are close to the surface of the body. Increased blood circulation brings more food and oxygen to the damaged tissue, helps remove waste products more efficiently, and thus aides the healing process.

Experience has shown that the use of heat is appropriate for minor strains and sore muscles. But heat alone is not very effective in preventing scar tissue formation, and is only marginally effective in treating pinched nerves, damaged ligaments and tendons, or damaged discs.

Physical therapists also use ice to treat swollen, aching injuries. Proper ice therapy, sometimes called cryotherapy, can be effective with many soft tissue injuries, especially when implemented shortly after the injury occurs. Ice therapy fosters healing by promoting increased blood circulation (even better than heat) and allows movement of the area by numbing pain sensation. Medical practitioners have found that the sooner an effective rehabilitation program is started, that includes movement of the injured area, the more healthy and supple the healed tissue will be. Movement promotes healing by increasing blood circulation and preventing the formation of scar tissue and adhesions.

With ice therapy, an effective rehabilitation program can begin as soon as the injured area can be moved. This can cut the recovery time dramatically, while still promoting the formation of healthy, quality tissue, rather than scar tissue.

Ice therapy must be used properly to reap its benefits and avoid aggravating the injury. The area should be chilled until it gets numb, usually five to 20 minutes. Once the area is numb, begin to move it, starting with small movements and gradually increasing your range of motion. Movement should be gentle, without putting weight on the injury. When the numbness wears off and the pain can be felt, reapply the ice and repeat the whole procedure.

While your body part is numb never attempt any strenuous activity. While muscles, ligaments, and tendons are cold, they are much less flexible than normal. If abnormally strained while cold they can be seriously injured. The pain may be numbed but the injury is still there — you could hurt yourself even more. Be sure to move your injured, numb body part gently and slowly.

Ice therapy is a safe and effective form of treatment, but as with any treatment, it is not recommended for all situations. There are some medical conditions (rheumatoid arthritis, allergy to cold, diabetes, or a rheumatic disease) which are not compatible with cryotherapy techniques. It is always a good idea to work with a trained medical professional in conjunction with any therapy.

Another treatment method physical therapists use is the relatively old healing art of deep massage. When skillfully done, massage can be a great aid in the healing process. There is a wide variety of massage techniques, each effective in its own way. Massage is most useful for muscle, tendon, or ligament strains and sprains, as well as soreness and swelling. In general, to be most effective with soft tissue injuries, massage should be done with a somewhat deep, penetrating pressure. Deep massage helps the healing process by increasing blood circulation in the affected area.

Massage also helps reduce general body tension which otherwise disrupts the healing process. When specific areas of the body are injured or in pain, other areas of the body compensate in ways which may lead to increased muscle tension and poorly aligned posture. These harmful physical side effects often continue long after an injury is healed. Deep massage can relieve this abnormal muscle tension and thus help restore the body to normal health.

Some massage techniques can even help break down abnormal scar tissue formed within muscles, ligaments, and tendons. When performed with controlled movement techniques, massage can also prevent or eliminate ligament-to-bone adhesions, thus allowing normal ligament healing to occur.

Deep massage is not directly helpful in cases of disc problems, nerve damage, severe ligament or tendon damage deep inside the body, or fractures. However, it is an excellent adjunct therapy to be used along with other treatment as these injuries heal.

The overall design of a particular physical therapy rehabilitation program is influenced by a number of factors including the type and severity of the injuries, the stage of healing, the restrictions of other treatments (surgery, medication, etc.), and the patient's health and strength. In fact, an effective rehabilitation program evolves as healing progresses. The use of exercise, heat, cold, and massage change as the injury heals.

Judy

Judy, and her husband Leonard, were returning home from the shopping mall on a Saturday afternoon. They were almost home, driving through their suburban section of town. Judy was in the back seat, breast feeding their new baby, when the car in front slammed on its brakes to avoid a child chasing a ball into the street. Leonard was paying more attention to Judy and the baby in the rearview mirror than he was to the road ahead. When he heard the screeching tires he had enough time to pull his foot off the accelerator but his foot never made it to the brake pedal.

There were shoulder straps in the back seat, which Judy was wearing, but no headrest. When the bumpers crushed together, Judy was propelled forward and then thrown back by the seat belt. Her head pivoted on the seat back, thrusting her neck forward as her head continued backward causing a classic whiplash injury. Judy also tried to protect the baby, enveloping it with her arms and upper thighs. As she thrust her right knee up, it shattered the hard plastic, metal framed ashtray on the seat back, aggravating an old knee injury.

She didn't feel much tension in her neck, initially. She was more frightened than in pain. Her knee was starting to swell and glow like an overripe tomato but Judy decided to wait a day or two before seeing the doctor. After all, her knee injury was a familiar one and so far there was just a little stiffness in her neck.

The baby's cries for food woke Judy up late that night. In a sleepy daze, she tried to lift her head off the pillow and was seized by jolts of pain radiating from her neck into her right shoulder and upper arm. Her neck muscles spasmed tightly. She needed Leonard to lift her to a sitting position. Once upright, Judy couldn't turn her head without turning her shoulders as well. The rest of the night crept by like a nightmare. She could barely feed the baby because any movement in her arms painfully strained her neck muscles. Her swollen, aching knee was an added annoyance she certainly did not need.

The next morning, her doctor explained that most moderate whiplash injuries are a combination of strained or torn ligaments and muscles. It often takes some time (up to a couple of days) for the physical trauma to become fully apparent. He suggested that Judy begin working with a physical therapist to rehabilitate the damaged tissue in her neck and knee, as quickly as possible. The doctor also strongly recommended that she try to avoid taking any pain medication because it could be passed along to the baby through her breastmilk.

Judy was surprised when her doctor recommended that she see a physical therapist. When she originally injured her knee she was told that rest and anti-inflammatory medication were the best thera-

pies. Although she felt that her knee was never as strong after the first injury, she expected similar advice this time.

The physical therapist immediately started Judy on an aggressive rehabilitation program. The therapist initially concentrated on reducing the muscle tension and pain in her neck and shoulder using ultrasound, ice, massage, and passive range of motion techniques. The therapist taught Judy several exercises and how to use ice properly, so she could continue the therapy at home.

The therapist primarily focused on reducing the swelling in Judy's knee with ice therapy. It was apparent that her previous knee injury had healed poorly, with a good deal of scar tissue. Their goal, once the swelling had subsided, was to use deep massage and ice therapy to dissolve the scar tissue, and heal the knee properly.

Over the course of the next few weeks Judy diligently used the techniques the physical therapist taught her. The physical therapist monitored her progress weekly, adjusting the tempo of her rehabilitation program according to the needs of her body. Within a month, she noticed a marked difference in her knee and leg strength. After three months of disciplined work with the physical therapist, Judy felt that her knee had healed to a better level than before the accident.

However, the progress healing her neck was not so smooth. After a few days of massage and ice therapy her muscle spasms subsided. But the stiffness in her neck and limited range of motion did not seem to improve over the next several weeks. Even though her neck muscles weren't quite so frozen, she still had a nagging pain in her right shoulder and arm. The physical therapist tried several massage and controlled movement techniques to loosen up Judy's neck with little success.

One day in the midst of this process, Judy was sharing accident stories with another patient in the physical therapist's office. Judy explained how frustrating it was to live with her neck disability. The other patient told Judy that she had hurt her lower back in an accident and walked around hunched over for almost a week before someone recommended that she visit a chiropractor. The other patient couldn't say enough about the chiropractic treatment. She believed that she would still be hobbling around like a woman three times her age if it hadn't been for the chiropractic therapy.

Judy was skeptical; neither her doctor or the physical therapist had even mentioned chiropractic treatment. But Judy figured anything was better than her current snail's pace progress. Breast feeding and sometimes even just holding her baby irritated her neck. She didn't want the baby's first experiences with her to be affected by her pain. Judy made an appointment to see a chiropractor the next day.

JOINT REALIGNMENT (CHIROPRACTIC OR OSTEOPATHIC MEDICINE)

Manipulation of the joints (normally done by a chiropractor or osteopath) can be an effective therapeutic component in the treatment of most injuries. Manipulation is the repositioning of the structural anatomy of the bones, tendons, ligaments, discs and cartilage to relieve musculoskeletal problems. Joint manipulation helps restore normal tissue alignment in the body, so that ligaments, tendons, muscles, or nerves are not squeezed, stretched, or irritated by abnormal alignment.

Chiropractic manipulation is especially useful when incorporated in a comprehensive rehabilitation program, to ensure that proper alignment is maintained during the healing process so that normal strength, flexibility, and range of motion are quickly restored. Manipulation techniques are particularly useful for whiplash and other spinal injuries.

Judy

Judy visited the chiropractor early the next morning. Not only did the chiropractic treatment help, but the chiropractor also explained to Judy some things she hadn't known about her body. He told Judy that the pain in her arm is called "referred pain." He explained that when some component of the spine, either soft tissue or bone, is injured (for example, a neck whiplash often causes strained or torn ligaments) the normal alignment of the area is disrupted. The structure of the spine is a complex web of nerves sprouting from the spinal column and vertebrae supported by ligaments, tendons, muscles, and discs. Even a tiny misalignment in this area can cause abnormal pressure on nerves (there are thirty-one pairs of spinal nerves) and also the spinal column itself. The result is muscle spasms, limited mobility, and PAIN.

Also, pressure on a spinal nerve can cause pain elsewhere in the body in a number of predictable patterns, not just in the limited area of the misalignment. For example, damage to ligaments at the very top of the spinal column causes pressure on the surrounding nerves. This, in turn, causes pain at the base of the jaw and the crown of the head, as well as pain in the neck itself. Damage to ligaments in the lower vertebrae (lumbar region) can cause pain in the legs and hips, even though those areas of the body are not damaged. The general pattern of pain is the same for most people and is based on neurological development that occurs in the womb. This pain felt in non-damaged areas is called "referred pain."

Considering the nature of her whiplash injury, the chiropractor explained that Judy's painful shoulder is probably due to damage to the ligaments supporting the 5th or 6th cervical (neck) vertebrae. The x-rays and physical exam confirmed the misalignment in this area.

To alleviate referred pain, and pain in the injured area itself, the obvious solution is to realign the bones and supporting structure of the spine. With the spine and supporting structure realigned, the excessive stress on the area is eliminated. And once the area is aligned, it is more likely that proper healing, without scar tissue and adhesions, will take place.

The chiropractor recommended that Judy continue her physical therapy sessions as well as the chiropractic treatment weekly. Once the manipulative therapy began, Judy's progress was dramatic. Although the severe tension had dissipated after the first few adjustments, she continued this treatment regime for several weeks. Once the structural anatomy of her spine was restored, the physical therapy exercises restored her strength and mobility quickly. Within twelve weeks her neck felt back to normal and she no longer had any discomfort in her shoulder or arm.

Judy's injuries were not as severe as they could have been. Her whiplash caused only minor ligament damage and spinal misalignment. In some cases, where minor misalignment is the root of an injury, chiropractic treatment alone can seem to work miracles. But when injuries include tissue damage, chiropractic manipulation should be accompanied by an aggressive rehabilitation program to maintain strength and promote healthy tissue growth.

ORTHOPEDIC SURGERY

The human body doesn't always come out the winner after ricocheting around the interior of a half-ton metal box on wheels that has gone out of control at 65 mph. The body is fantastically tough and resilient, but sometimes it hasn't a chance. When the motion finally stops, oftentimes there are broken bones, severely torn tendons and ligaments, and very deformed joints. These injuries require mechanical and/or surgical manipulation to initiate the healing process properly.

Breaks, tears, and misshapen joints need to be pinned, stapled, or otherwise set into place, usually by an orthopedic surgeon. Most of these severe injuries must be immobilized (with a cast or traction) in the initial stages of the healing process. For two to three weeks, protecting the injured area, sleeping, and eating properly are the best aid to healing. Rehabilitation can be extremely slow and demands patience and a positive attitude.

Although progress can be slow at first, it is still important to begin a rehabilitation program immediately. There are two things to consider when recovering from severe injuries: do not ignore the rest of your body while your injury is healing and do not ignore the associated soft tissue damage that often accompanies broken bones.

It is tempting to turn into a couch potato when you are carrying a ten pound plaster tube on your arm or leg. But your body needs exercise and activity. With exercise comes increased blood circulation which the damaged area especially needs. At first, very gentle isometrics, or a slow walk will do the trick. As the injury begins to heal you may be able to increase the activity somewhat. Also, you should pay close attention to maintaining flexibility and strength in the joints on either side of the injury. If you are in a cast, these joints are under additional stress both from the added weight of the cast and because you rely on them to buffer your fragile injury.

It is hard to imagine an instance where an accident could cause a bone to break without also damaging the adjacent soft tissue. A portion of the pain from the injury is probably due to bruised or torn muscles and tendons. Your rehabilitation program should attend to all the damaged tissue, not just the obvious broken bone.

The orthopedic reconstruction of broken bones or damaged joints is only the beginning of the healing process. It is particularly important if you are severely injured that you take advantage of the wide variety of rehabilitation techniques (discussed in this section) to accelerate your healing. The more severe your injury the more you need a comprehensive, full range of medical care.

ACUPUNCTURE

Acupuncture is a form of traditional Chinese medicine in which a number of very fine metal needles are inserted into the skin at specially designated points. The Chinese have used this technique for centuries in healing and pain relief. The acupuncture points (about 800) are arranged along 14 lines, called meridians, running the length of the body from head to foot. The traditional Chinese explanation for the effectiveness of acupuncture is based on the Taoist philosophy that good health depends on free circulation of T'chi, or life force energy, throughout the body. The meridians are the main channels of energy flow. Injury, stress, or disease impede the energy flow through the body. Acupuncturists believe that piercing the channels at the proper points helps correct the imbalance of energy flow. They believe that unrestricted energy flow has a curative effect.

It has also been suggested that acupuncture works by stimulating or repressing the autonomic nervous system in various ways. In particular, stimulation of the skin can affect internal organs and tissue by stimulating nerve reflex pathways to accelerate blood flow and healing.

Acupuncture can provide an excellent alternative to oral medication for pain relief.

Jolene

I was double-parked outside the post office fumbling with my mail and my seat belt. I was turned sideways looking in my purse when I was rear ended. The impact was relatively mild but I was thrown against the steering wheel at a very awkward angle. I really twisted my midback and bruised my ribs. Within a day, my midback felt extremely tense and stiff. Lifting paperwork, even deep breathing caused sharp pains in my ribs.

My doctor told me that my bruised ribs were best treated with tender loving care. He recommended that I take it easy until my aches subsided. What was unusual was that he was reluctant to prescribe muscle relaxants. Instead, he spent some time showing me the best way to use ice and controlled movements to regain my flexibility. He also recommended that I see an acupuncturist.

I was apprehensive about acupuncture treatment because I do not like needles. I had a hard time believing that using my body as a pincushion could relieve my pain. But I trusted my physician and decided to at least talk to an acupuncturist.

The acupuncturist assured me that the very fine tipped acupuncture needles felt nothing like the larger needles used for shots and blood samples. He was telling the truth, the acupuncture needles were so tiny, I barely felt them piercing my skin.

I thought the treatment was relatively uneventful; the acupuncturist put a number of needles into various points of my body and left them there for 15 or 20 minutes. Different areas on my body got warm with a slight tingling electricity. Some of the pain and discomfort in my back was replaced by a magnetic warmth.

For the first few days after my accident, I saw the acupuncturist daily. The pain didn't disappear altogether but I didn't have to deal with the dull, blurry feeling that comes with muscle relaxants or mild narcotics. After a few treatments, I could feel that my whole nervous system was stimulated slightly. It felt like the acupuncturist had turned up the dial on my body's healing machinery.

NONSURGICAL RECONSTRUCTIVE THERAPY

Nonsurgical reconstructive therapy, also referred to as prolotherapy, sclerotherapy or proliferative therapy, is especially effective for tendon or ligament damage. Torn or severely stretched ligaments and tendons generally do not heal well on their own because of the poor blood circulation in these tissues. Reconstructive therapy is the introduction of an irritant solution by means of injection into these damaged areas. The solution causes a slight, localized inflammation. The body responds by increasing the blood supply to the inflamed (injected) area. In effect, the body responds to irritation from the injected solution by laying down healthy tissue.

Nonsurgical reconstructive therapy is often effective where other treatments have failed. Proliferant therapy is attractive because unlike many drugs, the injected solutions have no side effects and stimulate the body to heal itself.

Paul

As I was backing out of my driveway one morning another car slammed into my passenger side. On impact my torso angled sharply sideways toward the passenger door. I could barely stand when I got out of the car. My lower and middle back muscles spasmed into a rigid block. Pain radiated into my groin and inner thigh.

My doctor said I probably had torn ligaments in my lower back. Over the next several months I was diligent in getting treatment. I visited a chiropractor biweekly and my physical therapist developed an aggressive rehabilitation program including exercise and deep massage. I was determined to regain my mobility and strength.

But getting rid of my lower back pain proved to be an elusive goal. The pain and tenderness diminished to a certain level and reached a plateau. Nine months after the accident I still felt protective of my back. Sometimes my lower back would ache like tit did a few days after the wreck, and the pain would spread to my inner thigh and groin.

On one particularly painful day, I was describing the inconsistency and nuisance of my symptoms to my attorney. He had heard similar stories before and gave me the name of an orthopedist who also performed reconstructive therapy. The orthopedist determined that my recurrent back pain was probably due to poorly healed ligaments.

I received a series of proliferant injections over a two month period. I also continued my weekly visits to the chiropractor while the proliferative injections did their work. By the time the injection series was complete, my pain had just about disappeared. For the next two months, I continued with physical therapy to build up strength in my lower back. It took about a year before I regained full agility, but I haven't experienced any problems since then.

Unfortunately, this form of therapy is not well known in the United States. But it is worth the investigation to find a practitioner who is familiar with this technique.

PHYSICAL AND EMOTIONAL HEALTH

Your automobile accident is potentially one of the more serious events in your life. It can be a time of extreme frustration; dealing with physical pain, economic worry, and the whole disruptive effect on your private and professional life. Needless to say, most of us have enough stress in our lives without the added trauma of an accident.

It is important to appreciate that dealing with stress and emotional discomfort can play a dramatic role in the healing process; physical and emotional health are integrally linked. One of the ways the human body expresses underlying emotional discomfort is through physical symptoms. Often, physical symptoms linger regardless of the physical treatment utilized, until the emotional upheaval of the accident is dealt with. Lingering headaches, stiff necks and backs, grinding teeth, and inexplicably slow healing might be symptoms of emotional adversity. Buried emotional trauma can even aggravate the intensity of injuries.

You do not have to live with your pain indefinitely, but you do have to listen to it in order to heal your wounds. The information in this chapter, on healing your physical trauma, is only a portion of what you need to know to heal from your accident. The following chapter is on emotional healing, an equally vital component in the healing process.

CONCLUSION

No doubt, the medical support necessary to heal your injuries is available, but you need to be aggressive in finding it. The information in this chapter can be used as a map to navigate the highway out of physical injury and pain, into health. As a reminder, some of the important approaches are:

- Learn to listen to your pain and trust your body's language.

- Be an active, diligent participant in your healing process.

- Document your progress in your Accident Log.

- Soft tissue damage can be painful and very debilitating. Do not ignore your physical pain just because you look fine on the outside.

- Try to find a primary caregiver who specializes in treating accident victims.

- Explore all the treatment options available. Do not become myopic or closed minded in your healing process.

- Your emotional well-being affects your physical body and the healing process. Healing the traumatic effects of an accident can be a very stress-filled process. Do not deny or ignore emotional discomfort.

- Have patience and believe in your body. If you provide it with the resources it needs to heal, it will likely find its way back to health.

NOTES

Chapter 5

PSYCHOLOGICAL TRAUMA

THE INVISIBLE INJURIES OF THE ACCIDENT TRAUMA

No matter what the circumstances—whether you were with friends or alone, at fault or just in the wrong place at the wrong time, injured or fortunate enough to walk away physically intact—being involved in a car accident is deeply upsetting and frightening. It is helpful if you imagine having two selves that can be injured in an accident (or any traumatic situation), a physical self and an emotional self. Generally, it is easy to see and feel physical wounds, they are the common measure of accident severity. Damage to your emotional or psychological self is less tangible, but it is your introspective, very personal eye that senses and feels this aspect of the accident injury.

Robin

There was no way anyone could have convinced me how frightening even a relatively minor accident can be. A friend had mentioned in passing that she had been involved in a fender bender but no one

77

had ever described how they felt and what they experienced. I normally felt so safe riding in my car and confident in my driving, I just never thought about what it would feel like to be in a crash.

I was broadsided on a residential street on a beautiful, sunny afternoon. Both of us were going about 25 miles-per-hour and I was wearing my seat belt so I was not thrown around too terribly much on impact. I saw the accident coming, so I had plenty of time to brace myself and anticipate. It took only a fraction of a second to wonder whether I might get killed. I was very, very scared. Even when I describe it now my heart skips a few beats and my stomach gets upset.

The other car hit the front driver's side of my car. The cars crushed together, my side of my car slapped into his passenger side like a book being slammed shut. The windows on my side shattered into my lap. That was really what I noticed first after we stopped bouncing; there was so much glass all over me. Then my teeth started chattering and wouldn't stop. I was so shocked, I don't think I blinked for two or three minutes.

I knew I was not hurt much physically, but as I think back now, I was emotionally shaken to my very core. It was a completely overwhelming sensory experience; there was so much noise, the screeching tires, the exploding glass, and the crushing of metal and plastic. As we slid side-by-side my stomach felt like it was floating in my chest as if I was on a wild, out of control roller coaster. Visually, it really seemed to happen in slow motion. I can close my eyes and replay those few moments just before and during impact in so much detail that I can remember the shock and surprise on the other driver's face *just before we collided. It was as if every cell in my body was awakened by the incredible fear aroused by the accident, every part of my body played a role in the horribleness of the experience.*

The other thing that really frightened me was seeing the bags of groceries that I had in the back seat strewn all over the car. There were broken eggs, ketchup, even oatmeal dust everywhere. I used to let my children ride in the backseat without seat belts. I hate to think what would have happened to them if they had been with me.

Although Robin's experience is only one out of an infinite variety of accident situations, being out of control in a metal and glass box naturally fires up a good dose of fear, anger, and helplessness.

On top of the burden of psychological distress stemming from the accident itself, additional emotionally troubling freight can come from a variety of sources throughout the recovery process. You might feel burdened from dealing with your physical injuries and the abnormal limitations they impose on your life. Economic recovery can also bring more than its fair share of frustration. The added anxiety from all sources can put a big strain on you and your personal relationships. Some degree of emotional upheaval is expected and normal. Just being aware of and sensitive to the extra emotional cargo the accident forces into your life is a giant step in initiating the healing process.

THE ACCIDENT TRAUMA: SORTING OUT THE PSYCHOLOGICAL IMPACT

It is the drama of the accident experience itself; the intensely potent feelings that are stirred up in those few moments of terrifying primal fear, when you are out of control and your life is seriously threatened, that can undermine psychological well-being. Similar to the spectrum of physical wounds, the range and intensity of psychological injuries caused by vehicle accidents falls on a continuum, from mild upset to severe cases of post-traumatic stress disorder. While each person will have their own unique experience in responding to an accident trauma, there are characteristics common to all.

YOUR INITIAL REACTION: SHOCK AND DENIAL

It is unlikely that you were emotionally prepared to have an accident. Even knowing intellectually how often accidents occur, you can't help but think it will happen to someone else. An impaired or inattentive driver can shatter that illusion in seconds. During the first few hours or even days after the accident, you can expect to struggle with the question, "Why me?" It is a question without a good answer. You might try to minimize or ignore how terrifying the accident was and how shocked and vulnerable you feel because it did happen to you.

Psychologists call this type of psychological defense mechanism "**denial**." It is a common way we humans deal with emotional upset. Initially the tendency is to deny, or at least minimize the fear, shock, and anger associated with an accident and to continue life as usual. Be clear, it is not that the emotions are not present, but that you try to act like an ostrich with its head in the sand, believing that if you don't consciously acknowledge or feel them, they do not exist.

SHOCK AND THE FIGHT-OR-FLIGHT RESPONSE

An accident is scary and stirs up a lot of mental and physical turmoil. Think about how your body automatically responds when you are frightened and angry: you feel your pulse in your neck and gut, your skin gets warm and flush with blood, you sweat, your muscles feel tensed and ready to move. Whenever you are confronted with a physically and/or emotionally threatening situation your nervous system answers physiologically with a massive release of hormones, in what is called the fight-or-flight or stress response.

When confronted, your mind evaluates the situation and if it decides you are threatened, it hormonally tells your body to get ready; in some manner it might need to fight or run. This psychophysiological reaction causes an increased heart rate, exaggerated breathing, enhanced blood supply to active muscles and decreased blood flow to organs that are not needed in the stress response, amplified cellular metabolism for energy, and magnified mental alertness. The mind also can cause a time expansion (slow motion) effect and sensory focus in which images are burned into memory.

An automobile accident, even a relatively minor one, can be unusually threatening and frightening. Until the glass settles, you do not really know how menacing or serious it may be. Generally, your mind/body prepares for the worst with its waterfall of hormones, giving you the critical muscular and mental alertness you need to react protectively. The heated psychophysiological response to the drama of the accident is an instinctive and deeply felt emotional and physical experience.

After the threat is removed, your conscious mind defends itself from feelings of intense fear and loss of control by denying or minimizing the incident. In a sense, your body conspires in the illusion because your nervous system's hyperarousal calms as well, and the physiologically altered state slowly fades. Your heart rate returns to normal, you aren't tensed for action; your body tells you the danger is gone, and it is time to move on to other things. However, physiologically, this is not the end of the fight-or-flight response. Once the stressful event ends and the body calms down, the impressive chemical response takes a toll. For example, the residual effects of the hormones cause your body to retain fluids for a time. When this happens you will need to urinate frequently or even experience prolonged diarrhea. Also, you may feel physically weak and sapped of energy, both as a result of the fluid loss and the "let-down" from the hormonal high you experienced. It may take several days before your biochemical balance returns to normal.

Understandably, you might respond by trying to convince yourself that the accident was really no "big deal," especially if you weren't badly hurt physically. You figure if you try to be strong, not feel the painful emotions, you will master the experience. In fact, denial can be so powerful a defense, you may have trouble remembering details of the accident. In some cases the whole experience cannot be recalled. Some experts believe that the memory block is partially attributable to the dramatic hormonal changes that coincide with the fight-or-flight response. They believe that conscious memory and recall is linked to the physiological state of the body at the time of the experience. During the traumatic experience, the body is in an abnormal (as compared to the everyday, relaxed) biochemical state. And in some complex fashion, the mind links the internally aroused biochemical environment with the memory of the event. The memory fades from conscious awareness as the body returns to its normal physiological state. Whatever the mechanisms, it is apparent that the brain is very sophisticated at protecting you from consciously feeling threatening emotions.

What is important for you to realize is the unconscious mind never forgets; the fear associated with the accident continues to brew. It takes a considerable amount of energy to deny and suppress the roots of fear and helplessness associated with the accident experience. Even if the conscious mind denies the feelings, they don't go away. Rather, they remain only partially buried.

AFTER SHOCK COMES THE EMOTIONAL UPHEAVAL

Shock and denial may last a few days or a few weeks. Some people quickly pass through the shock phase and feel the psychological jolt of the accident within a day or two. For others, the emotional aftereffects are like simmering stew, the full flavor, depth, and strength develop more potently with time. Initially, it is not unusual to bounce back and forth between the two responses, one moment thinking "no big deal, life goes on," and the next, experiencing fountains of uncomfortable emotions and physical symptoms.

Jean

Jean was driving a passenger van on a two lane highway, taking a group from her church to a picnic spot in a nearby rural area. Jean lost control of the van when a tire blew-out. The van flipped onto its side and skidded about 50 feet, coming to rest in the dirt beside the road. Miraculously, all but one passenger was wearing a seat belt; most of the injuries were limited to bruises and cracked ribs. Jean suffered only a few scratches and bruises. But the one man not wearing a seat belt was violently thrown about the cab and died later that day from the head injuries he sustained.

At first Jean was numb and dazed by the whole experience. She felt like it was someone else, certainly not her, who was involved in the accident. She felt detached, as though the experience was a dream and she would wake up, scared but safe in her own bed. The man who died in the accident was only an acquaintance, so at first she had only a mild emotional reaction to his death.

The accident was on a Friday afternoon; Jean slept through the whole weekend. It was as if the accident totally drained her body of all its energy, leaving her in a numbed stupor. By Monday morning she was rested enough to go to work. She made it until lunch before she started to realize the enormity of what had taken place over the weekend.

As she was typing, in her mind's eye she would have momentary visual glimpses of different aspects of the accident scene. The overwhelming numbness was slowly fading and she started to connect to how frightening the accident actually was. At first she would just shake her head and thank God for how lucky she was to be safe.

Later that afternoon, the realization that a man had died in the accident struck the bottom of her soul. A warm, sad shower of grief washed over her. She left work and had a good long cry over the experience, letting her tears drain the fear and sadness from her body.

During the first few weeks following the accident, as your body calms and you emotionally and intellectually come to recognize the size of the ordeal you experienced, you may feel, to some degree, as if you are on an emotional roller coaster, riding bumpy curves and loops of anxiety, discomfort, confusion, depression, anger, grief, sadness, and fear. The sudden, unexpected terror of being helpless, out of control, and threatened by serious injury or death shakes the roots of your internal sense of safety and well-being.

Also, the accident experience can be especially shocking because most of us feel relatively safe and protected in automobiles — a car often feels like a second home. The accident shatters that image of comfort and safety, replacing it with a pervasive sense of fear and vulnerability.

There are a variety of factors which influence your emotional response to a traumatic situation. Some of these factors will be explored but it is beyond the scope of this chapter to cover all of them. It is more important to appreciate the circumstances of your accident and that a traumatic experience can inflict psychological damage. The severity of injury covers a wide spectrum from mild emotional upset to devastating post-traumatic stress disorder (PTSD). Clearly, each individual responds differently, but for simplicity, we will divide the spectrum of psychological injury into three categories: mild, moderate, and severe injury.

The following discussion of these three groups and their characteristic symptoms are meant to help you understand how psychological injury manifests itself and to give you a rough indication of the depth of your injury. Regardless of where you fit on this continuum, remember you are not alone. This information is the product of many tears and countless hours of grieving by other accident victims. Once you recognize that a wound exists, you can take steps to heal it.

SUFFERING MILD UPSET

Regardless of whether physical injuries are present, or how badly damaged the vehicles may be, the baseline emotion associated with all accidents is fear. The experience is similar to a mugging or other violent crime in the sense that you lose control over your well-being and are truly victimized and helpless for a time. Undoubtedly, most people like to feel in control, to have power and choice over the situations in their life. It is terribly unsettling and frightening when that control is taken away. Along with fear, you might readily respond with anger or even rage (helpless anger).

It is not that you feel no emotional impact from the accident with a mild injury. To the contrary, even those who are not significantly traumatized feel the full range of fear and anger accompanying the experience. It is natural to feel angry at the other driver, at the incredible inconvenience of the whole process, and at the insensitivity of the "system."

Tim

I was stopped at a red light, on my commute home from my office, when I was rear-ended by a drunk driver. The wreck was like being struck by lightning, it was over almost before I understood what was happening. Luckily, I was wearing my seat beat and the other car wasn't going too fast. My head was whipped backward then forward on impact. My neck muscles started to stiffen and spasm almost immediately.

The other driver was slightly dazed and disoriented; I could smell the liquor on his breath. It took every ounce of control I could muster not to scream at him. The crash just shouldn't have happened. Because this stupid man got into his car drunk, I was in pain and had to deal with this incredible inconvenience.

Over the next several weeks, I got a real appreciation for the enormity of impact this relatively minor wreck created. For the first few weeks I felt irritable and short-tempered because I was in constant pain from the neck whiplash. Normally, when I was emotionally tense, I would go for a jog or play racquetball, but now physical activity was out of the question. I was scared that my neck would not heal properly and that I would never be able to resume my regular lifestyle. Sometimes I felt like I was overflowing with anger and confusion because of the painful disability and the senselessness of the crash.

Occasionally, the pain would get me thinking about the details of the incident. At times I would imagine different scenarios; if I hadn't been wearing a seat belt I would be a bloody mess. Or if the drunk driver had been going faster, my neck may have been more severely damaged or I might have been paralyzed. The fantasies allowed me to get in touch with how the accident experience made me feel so frightened and out of control. It was the first time in my life I felt truly victimized and helpless. It was not a comfortable feeling.

After the crash I became what I thought of as a nervous driver. Sometimes I felt like I was more attentive to the cars in my rearview mirror, because I was rear-ended, than to the oncoming traffic. Slowly, as my neck healed and I was able to resume my normal routine, I regained my confidence driving.

To some degree, I felt that the crash experience was an emotional scar that might never heal. The drunk driver received a fine and a minimal license suspension, while I spent 6 months rehabilitating my neck.

Tears, some screaming in anger and frustration (whether internally or out loud), even some depression or apathy are normal emotional reactions. Perhaps what characterizes a mild trauma best is that the emotional impact is relatively easy to manage. With a more mild level of injury, consciously feeling and giving voice to all the emotions associated with the accident might be upsetting but it doesn't feel bigger than life. Certainly, even a minor wreck can throw a life-size curve even athletes would have trouble with, but with a mild trauma you can respond by actively making space for, and adjustments to, your changing circumstances and emotions.

Other symptoms that characterize a mild reaction are feeling anxious while driving (like after the first time you fell off your bicycle), being more edgy, restless, and irritable. Again, these are expected and relatively mild reactions to the shock of the experience and the added stress of dealing with the police, medical professionals, insurance companies, and lawyers. Generally, these stress symptoms dissipate with time, support from those around you, and completion of the physical and economic healing processes.

SUFFERING MODERATE DISTRESS

For some of you, the terror of the experience might reach more deeply and linger more substantially in your psyche. With a moderate injury you might feel apprehensive about driving or riding in a car, and be unusually protective. The additional tension of the accident wears heavily on your shoulders, influencing almost every aspect of your life.

Try as you might, with a moderate injury you cannot pull yourself back to normal by denying the impact of the experience because it leaks into your conscious life. Your personal relationships may become strained. When expressing anger or hurt you react more strongly than appropriate; you feel unusually tired, apathetic, or depressed. In many ways, the stress symptoms are similar to those experienced by those who are mildly affected, but the magnitude differs noticeably.

Some experts have found that some who experience symptoms of a moderate injury have a background or prior life experience of trauma which has not been dealt with fully. Over the years, the memories and emotions linked to the prior trauma have been locked away behind the door in one of the mind's dark closets. Remember, denial is a powerful defense mechanism. But the unrelated trauma of the accident puts you into an emotional state of fear, anxiety, and helplessness, along with the simultaneous physiological fight-or-flight response common to all trauma. It is a reversal of the mechanism of memory loss discussed earlier in this chapter. In this case, the similar psychophysiological state acts as a catalyst, unlocking and letting loose the floodgates of the similar but suppressed feelings of the original trauma. As remarkable as it may seem, it is not uncommon for an automobile accident to trigger long suppressed memories of child abuse (the unconscious mind is extremely efficient at protecting children from consciously carrying painful experiences), sexual abuse, or other painfully traumatic events. The combined emotional turmoil of the accident and the previously suppressed trauma snowball into a disproportionate mass of fear, hurt, and anger. As you can imagine, the emotional force of this type of experience can be quite strong.

Moderate psychological injury is also manifested in physical symptoms. It is as if the psychological trauma and deeply felt fear has a physical component which infects the body. The symptoms might include chronic headaches, stomach or digestive trouble, intensification of previous medical problems, or enigmatic physical pain. The psychological wound can even hinder the normal healing process of physical injuries.

With a moderate psychological trauma, you might find that you sometimes have trouble concentrating on normal activities. Instead, you find yourself dwelling on the accident. You might run the scene over and over in your mind, imagining more severe injuries, different outcomes, or even your own death. Screeching tires, shattering glass, driving by the accident scene, or anything else that is reminiscent of the accident causes an increase in anxiety and is abnormally unsettling.

Sleep patterns can also be disrupted. Violent, fear-filled nightmares that recreate the helpless and out of control feelings experienced in the accident are common. Once restful sleep is compromised; the already distressing symptoms are further aggravated. Patience wears thin and relationships suffer, anxiety approaches the "red alert" level, and most important, physical healing will not occur without proper sleep.

When added to the discomfort of the moderate psychological injury, the stress and inconvenience of taking care of the medical and economic fallout of the accident can become monumental. Each step of the supposed recovery process seems to take more energy than is restored. Rather than feeling as if the worst of the experience is over with the clearing of the accident scene, it feels as if the emotional toll increases with time and effort. So much emotional energy is tied up with the experience and the adversity of symptoms, the tendency is to feel further victimized by the whole process.

Roger

> *I was rear-ended on a busy freeway. It didn't seem like a very serious accident; my knee hurt from hitting the dashboard and my neck was strained a bit, but no one else was hurt and the cars were still mobile. Yet, everything seemed to add up to a very startling experience: the accident itself was so abrupt it just came out of nowhere. The other driver was belligerent and intimidating even though it was his fault. My boss was furious that I wrecked the company car. Even the police officers were cold and disinterested. I don't remember feeling scared, now I think I was really in shock, but I remember wanting to run away as far and as fast as I could.*

> *I figured the accident would quickly fade into a lousy memory, but I was wrong. The headaches*

started on the first night. My doctor gave me Valium and I was probably mildly drugged for over three months because my body just did not want to loosen up. My head hurt almost continually, my neck was stiff, and my knee was taking forever to get better.

It seemed like I was doing all the right things. I was following the directions of the physical therapist, as best I could, but I could tell he was frustrated because my body just wasn't responding to the treatment in the way he expected. My own frustration started to show itself at work and with my family. No one seemed to understand or accept that I was in pain; I looked healthy but I just couldn't do the things I normally did. It became such a giant snowball of frustration, physical pain, and lack of energy that I felt completely alienated from the people and things I cared for.

I explained how frustrated and alone I was feeling to my doctor and luckily he understood what was going on. He suggested that I see a psychologist. He told me that my headaches and lack of progress healing physically are classic symptoms of emotional trauma.

I had never really talked to anyone about the accident itself, or at least how it felt. Once I started talking about how startled and out of control I felt the emotions seemed to wash over me out of nowhere. I guess they were always there, but I never even thought to talk to anyone about the experience. I never gave the emotions the space to come up before. At one point, I actually cried for the first time in probably 10 years.

The most remarkable aspect of the psychotherapy process was that I learned I have been carrying a lifetime, over 40 years, of hurt and anger. I just never learned to express that part of me. I grew up in an abusive home. My father was a strict disciplinarian, he used to beat me fairly often, usually for reasons I never understood. In a very real way, the accident made me feel just like I did when my father hit me — the violent abruptness, the total out of control feeling, and the intimidating anger of the other driver — it was like I was five years old and at the mercy of my father. I was in complete terror and wanted to run but couldn't.

The accident stirred up all those old, buried feelings that as a child I didn't have any idea how to deal with. As an adult, I only dimly remembered that my father was an angry, unhappy man. Once I started to talk about all the feelings I realized the extent of the abuse I experienced as a child. No wonder I had headaches and my body wasn't healing. There were forty years of tears in the way.

Once I started talking, or rather expressing my feelings in a constructive way, my progress was miraculous. Within a month the headaches were gone. My whole body seemed to relax and heal.

While these symptoms seem dramatic, they are not unusual or a result of the most severe injury. If your sleep is affected for any length of time, or headaches or other unfamiliar physical pain persists, your body and unconscious mind may be asking for help. On an unconscious level, it may be you are having trouble dealing with the accident. Of course, it is your choice how you live with the discomfort — no doubt you can accommodate a good deal of pain and discomfort in your life — but there is no reason to passively accept and endure these symptoms of emotional injury.

SUFFERING SEVERE TRAUMA: POST-TRAUMATIC STRESS DISORDER

In this category of injury, the accident not only damages cars and bodies, but emotional well-being as well. With this level of psychological trauma, the accident will leave you feeling alone, very helpless, and emotionally disabled. Your "normal" routine is disrupted by nightmares, jumpiness, difficulty in concentrating, headaches, and extreme anxiety when driving or riding in an automobile. Again, the symptoms on this end of the distress continuum are similar to those characteristic of mild or moderate injuries, but the degree, the intensity, and the disabling effects are much more extreme.

The specific cluster of prolonged psychological and physiological symptoms associated with severe trauma is now known as post-traumatic stress disorder (PTSD). PTSD was first diagnosed among persons in military combat, but it is now known to affect people who have either been a victim of, or witness to, any significant psychologically distressing event, including a car accident.

In 1980 the American Psychiatric Association formally recognized PTSD. In its *Diagnostic and Statistical Manual of Mental Disorders (DSM-III)*, PTSD is now defined as a behavioral disorder which can occur "following a psychologically distressing event that is outside the range of usual human experience." The "trigger" or "stressor" event is also one which "would be markedly distressing to almost anyone and is usually experienced with intense fear, terror, and helplessness."

The *DSM-III* presents a wide variety of stressors which might trigger PTSD. The event commonly involves a serious threat to life, and automobile accidents certainly fit the bill. It is now accepted that natural disasters (earthquakes, floods, fires, etc.) as well as human-made situations (airplane crashes, automobile accidents, hostage situations, wars, etc.) are all events which pack sufficient psychological punch to induce PTSD.

The psychiatric definition is purposely broad because it is not understood why, given similar stressor events, some will develop PTSD and others will not. Thus far, experts have not identified a factor which might significantly influence the probability of developing PTSD. Probably the propensity towards PTSD involves a number of factors, including prior psychological and physical health, heredity, and the ability to acknowledge and talk about feelings surrounding the event, along with the type, severity, and duration of the traumatic event. Surprisingly, a physical injury is not essential in developing PTSD; the event need only be psychologically traumatizing.

It is true that life offers some dramatic, overwhelmingly gut-wrenching experiences, like automobile accidents. Certainly you cope with these situations and the very strong emotions they inspire as best you can. But sometimes the trauma can be emotionally overwhelming, cracking the internal mantle of well-being that you normally protect and nourish. Sometimes, particularly when a person does not live in an emotionally supportive environment, the normal coping mechanisms can fail. The resulting internal disharmony can lead to the prolonged and disabling emotional and physical symptoms of PTSD.

The American Psychiatric Association groups the symptoms of PTSD in three characteristic clusters. First is the tendency to relive the traumatic event in nightmares, flashback episodes, intrusive, vivid images and recollections, and to feel intense emotional distress when exposed to situations that symbolize the trauma. The second cluster of symptoms is characterized by a numbed emotional state, a generalized detachment and disinterest, and extreme avoidance of activities, thoughts, or feelings associated with the shock. The final cluster is characterized by what is called hyperarousal, which includes difficulty sleeping, irritability and hostility, difficulty concentrating, and hyperphysiological response when exposed to events that symbolize aspects of the trauma.

Catherine

The troubling symptoms seemed to intensify for Catherine over the course of about four weeks following the accident. The nightmares started the day after the accident, the first occurring when she had fallen asleep on the physical therapist's work table. In this nightmare, she relived the terror of the accident. Her screams startled everyone in the office, including herself. The nightmares continued almost every time she tried to sleep. At first they were a straightforward replay of different aspects of the accident. She would always wake up sweating and short of breath, or if they were particularly frightening she would wake up screaming. She started to sleep in a separate bedroom because her nightmares woke her husband up as well.

By the end of the week she was afraid to go to sleep. At best she slept two or three hours a day. Understandably, she was always tired and edgy. Her physical symptoms were exacerbated by the lack of sleep. During that time she also developed diarrhea which persisted on and off for several weeks. Anytime she got slightly nervous her mouth would go completely dry, so dry it felt like she had to rip her lips apart to talk. Sudden noises or unexpected movement startled her as if she was continually expecting something threatening to occur.

Prior to the accident, she and her husband ran a small business, but now Catherine was unable to work. Even the most menial task, like sitting in a chair or carrying a bag of groceries, was almost impossible because of her whiplash and strained back. They had to hire someone to replace Catherine in their business and her husband had to do the work of two around the house. At first, he really did not understand why Catherine was so dramatically affected by the accident — her car was severely damaged, but she looked okay from the outside (she had only soft tissue injuries) — so he became resentful and impatient because of all the extra work and financial burden he had to assume.

Catherine stayed in the house for the first two weeks, only leaving to go to the doctor or the physical therapist. She even had trouble walking her dog because the tugs on the leash would painfully jar her neck and back.

During this time she started to notice that she would occasionally go into a sort of trance, losing track of time. Once she found herself "coming awake" standing at the sink and realized she had been there for over a half-hour in a semi-catatonic state. Another time, she came awake standing in the park with her dog at her feet. She realized she must have been in the trance for forty-five minutes, the time it usually took for her dog to tire from chasing birds. During some of these trances, she could sort of remember seeing video tapes of the accident or other violent situations in her mind, but other trances were a total blank. Sometimes it felt as if she was having her nightmares while she was awake.

Catherine always thought of herself as a very social and outgoing person but now felt nervous or afraid in normal situations. She felt as if she was losing control of her life and at times, her mind. She tried to maintain some part of her normal routine. Even though it was terrifying, she forced herself to drive.

When she did her whole body would tense, by the end of a 10 mile drive she would be drenched with perspiration. Freeway driving was totally out of the question, she was scared of everyone on the road.

Her wild, horrible nightmares started to grow from violent accident scenes to men chasing her and trying to hurt her. Always the central theme was a feeling of being threatened, terrified, and out of control.

It is important to note that the combination of symptoms and their severity vary. The intensity of PTSD itself falls on a continuum, from relatively mild symptoms to considerable emotional disruption. Even with fairly extreme symptoms, you may not recognize you have a problem. Instead, you might attempt to adjust your life to the symptoms and deny any discomfort as best you can.

PTSD symptoms are often self-perpetuating and self-aggravating, following a predictable cyclical pattern. The cycle might start with physical pain, emotional discomfort, or a symbolic event in the environment that is reminiscent of the trauma of the accident. This triggers visual images, thoughts, or flashback memories of the incident which causes an increase in autonomic nervous system activity. Reliving the trauma through these flashbacks causes the body to respond physiologically as though the trauma is reoccurring, actually causing a fight-or-flight response. This increased anxiety aggravates the physical and emotional discomfort, intensifying the recall of the trauma. The painful cycle of PTSD continues.

Although the spiral might be initiated by events in the environment, once the cycle is set in motion, environmental circumstances actually fade into the background. Like a needle stuck in the groove of a scratched record, the continuous loop between the mind's recollection of the event, the induced surges of anxiety, and aggravated physical symptoms maintains the spiraling effect of the stress disorder independent of a triggering event.

The onset of symptoms may be immediate, gradual, or as has been the case for some, not develop for a period of time. Onset depends to some degree on how unremittingly the painful emotions are consciously suppressed. When intense emotions like grief, sadness, anger, and remorse are held inside over some period, they can turn into a formidable internal force. If this emotional turmoil is not addressed directly, it can transform into PTSD.

A few words of caution: you might be tempted to "self-medicate" the symptoms away, using alcohol and/or drugs to numb your pain. With PTSD, this form of substance abuse is like adding lead weight to a sinking ship, pushing you deeper and deeper into a cycle of pain and alienation. Over a period of time, it requires more and more energy to remain numb, which means more and more drugs or alcohol. As the abuse increases, you have less and less energy available to invest in a healthy life. In these cases, the substance abuse adds a new layer of disease to an already complex and highly confused emotional state and makes proper diagnosis and treatment much more difficult.

THE CIRCUMSTANCES SURROUNDING THE ACCIDENT

Although most psychological reactions depend on subjective perception of the accident (i.e., it depends on how fearful and out of control you felt rather than on any external objective criteria) some accidents are more perilous and provide more shock potential than others. If there were fatalities or serious injuries you may be more affected. If you were involved in a very dramatic accident you may feel that you have a legitimate reason to be upset. Thus you probably would not deny your discomfort and are more likely to talk about how you were affected and less reluctant in getting professional help.

In contrast, it is the less dramatic, but oftentimes equally frightening situation that can cause the most long-lasting trouble. These are the accidents which leave a person with soft-tissue injuries but no externally apparent physical wounds. An accident may have been quite brutal, but if you look in the mirror and look fine, you think you should feel as normal as you look. All your pain, both physical and emotional, lies below the skin. In these situations, you might tend to deny the symptoms and try to push your discomfort away. The emotional turmoil can fester in your subconscious and you might wait to do something about your suffering until the symptoms become acute and unbearable.

Small details about the accident can also have a disproportionate effect on you. If you were alone in your car and/or the other driver threatened or intimidated you, it can intensify your fear. If the other driver was uncooperative or did not speak the same language as you, if young children were affected, it can magnify your feelings of helplessness. When you are in the midst of the fight-or-flight hormonal response, your body is cued to notice and react to nuances in the environment and your mind's role is to dramatize all these circumstances. Often, it is the little things which stand out in your memory and tend to be the emotional focal point of the accident.

Barbara

I was knocked out of control on the freeway by a truck changing lanes. I spun around in two or three circles and came to rest against the center divider facing the oncoming traffic. Once stopped, I sat in my car, in shock, for what seemed like hours, until someone stopped to help me. Afterwards, whenever I thought of the accident, I would remember how utterly isolated and alone I felt sitting in my car facing the oncoming traffic, as I met the eyes of driver after driver who passed me by. I felt like a lost child in a department store with no one willing to stop and help.

CONCLUSION

Unfortunately, most people never consider the emotional wounds that result from an automobile accident. Psychological well-being is an area which most people overlook or take for granted. Your emotional health is a valuable personal possession. Psychological wounds are as real and as treatable as physical injuries. The information in this chapter is meant to better define the potential psychological trauma of an automobile accident so you can look at your own experience with greater understanding. Some of the important considerations are:

- Whether you are consciously in touch with the feelings or not, a violent car accident is a whole mind/body experience, arousing a good deal of fear and a strong physiological fight-or-flight response.

- The fear, helplessness, and lack of control experienced during the accident can be a poisonous influence on your emotional integrity.

- Emotional trauma manifests itself in a variety of debilitating physical and psychological symptoms.

- Psychological injuries can significantly disrupt the physical healing process.

Chapter 6

PSYCHOLOGICAL RECOVERY

EMOTIONAL RESOLUTION AND HEALING

From a broad view, your accident experience is not over until you heal emotionally, as well as physically, and economically. In the same way that your physical body needs time and nurturing to heal properly, so, too, does your emotional self. Given the appropriate attention and care, you will find that, emotionally, you have the same innate ability to heal as you do physically.

THE HEALING POWER OF LETTING YOUR FEELINGS TELL THEIR STORY

To mend your psychological injury, the most nurturing and healing thing you can do is give your feelings a voice, let them tell their story. When feelings are not consciously acknowledged and expressed they do not disappear. They won't show on an x-ray but they influence your physical and emotional health.

The emotions the crash inspired — fear, anger, sadness, guilt, and helplessness — are quite real. During the accident you did not have time nor the opportunity to give them proper attention. Yet, to varying degrees, these intense emotions are present. Remember your first teenage crush, how overpowering and all consuming the infatuation felt? You could sense the presence of the feelings in your whole body. It was as if they had weight and substance. Just as love, laughter, and joy can fill you with health, unresolved fear, anger, and helplessness can pollute you with dis-ease.

Cleansing your emotional wounds by letting your feelings tell their story is not a complex process. Nevertheless, considering the emotional content of the original experience, it can be painful. This process is called grieving. Psychic wounds heal naturally when you allow yourself to grieve over the trauma. Grieving helps you remove the unhealthy charge of the trauma by acknowledging the full range of emotions as real, a part of your experience. Until the emotions are given expression, you are denying that part of yourself which remains suppressed and ignored. Part of you is isolated as sort of a frozen emotional energy block. You validate and legitimize the feelings of the experience by allowing yourself to feel and integrate them as part of yourself. When you consciously acknowledge the feelings associated with the accident they lose their destructive potency.

CHOOSING THE CORRECT ENVIRONMENT TO TELL YOUR STORY AND GRIEVE

An important part of grieving is telling your story in the appropriate environment. It is very difficult to validate and give expression to your feelings without wholesome support. Most of you know and practice this process intuitively. You talk over your experiences with friends or other confidants. Sharing your life in this way is natural and life-giving. Done in the context of the accident experience, the cold, fragmenting power of fear and helplessness lose their unhealthy effect. This is particularly true when the emotional content of the experience is re-lived and released in a supportive environment. Whether you choose to do this with loved ones, a medical practitioner, or a professional counselor depends somewhat on the severity of your symptoms.

IF YOU HAVE MILD SYMPTOMS

If you are only mildly effected by the accident the important thing is that you don't ignore your feelings. Even if your symptoms are relatively mild in that you are only a little irritable or slightly apprehensive driving, make the time to reflect on the feeling content of your accident experience. Your task is to find the situation that feels safe enough for you to explore the emotional content of the accident experience. You need to get, and give yourself, the support and validation necessary for healing to occur.

You might do this with a friend, a spouse, a professional, or anyone else you trust. The important thing is for you to feel safe enough to express your feelings. If you do choose a non-professional, make sure he or she knows what you want. You need their undivided attention and support to tell your story, to grieve. Make sure you will not be interrupted and that the person understands that this is your time to relate your accident experience.

As you talk through the accident experience, focus on your body and your emotions. Feel the experience and let it all come up, especially the tears and fear and anger. You might find that your heart rate increases, you get butter-flies in your stomach, and you sense some of the other physical symptoms of the fight-or-flight response. It is all part of re-living and relieving the experience. Again, just let it all come out. Shout, cry, jump around, whatever it takes so that you don't hold it in your body any more. Because of the emotions that can come up, you want to make sure you feel comfortable in the physical setting as well.

IF YOU HAVE MODERATE SYMPTOMS

If your symptoms fall in this area (bad nightmares, high anxiety or depression, for example) your body is demanding that you pay attention. For you, the worst four words in the English language are, "it will go away." For you, it is not appropriate to pretend nothing is wrong and hope that time will wash away the experience.

All the suggestions written above for those with mild symptoms apply to you, but more so. You need to make time to work through the emotional content of the accident. If your symptoms are on the mild side of moderate, you are probably fine working with a friend or your spouse. Otherwise seek professional help. If your symptoms persist or worsen, you owe it to yourself to get professional attention.

In whatever manner you decided to establish your grieving process, you can expect that it will take some time. Remember that you have an innate mechanism that will steer you to health if you allow the time and nurturing necessary.

John

Although I wasn't really hurt — I had a mild concussion and some cuts and bruises — I think the experience was so overwhelming I shifted into a numbed, robotic state right after the accident. I know I never lost consciousness; I actually helped pull the truck driver from his cab and apparently gave the police a full account of the wreck before I went to the emergency room. But by morning the experience was a hazy, fragmented memory.

Almost immediately I knew that the accident effected me deeply. I don't think I ever really calmed down or returned to normal. Within a few days I started having trouble sleeping, and within a week

I started having unexplained stomach aches. My chiropractor suggested I see a therapist because he felt my muscles were actually getting more tense over time rather than loosening up.

After a few preliminary sessions, the therapist used hypnosis to help me consciously reconnect to the intense emotional trauma of the experience. I think I had trouble remembering the details because they were just too painful and terrifying. The safety of the therapeutic setting and power of hypnosis was the combination I needed emotionally to come to terms with the experience.

Hypnosis helped put me in a psychological state where I could remember the whole accident. I was able to connect with the fear and helplessness I had suppressed and to physically release it from my body. It sounds odd, but that is really what I did; as I moved through the accident experience while in the hypnotic trance, I could physically feel the tension of intense fear being released from my stomach and my shoulders.

Once the emotional fury of the experience was drained I felt as if clamps were removed from my muscles. I still needed my physical rehabilitation program but my healing was no longer impeded by the emotional trauma related to the accident.

Depending on your personal circumstances, you may want to explain what is happening in your life to your employer, family, and your close friends. Particularly if you were not physically injured or had only soft tissue injuries it can help everyone understand that you have an extra load of stress in your life. It will help maintain your relationships if friends understand why you are anxious or irritable. If you acknowledge on a feeling level how the accident impacted your life, the burden will be less weighty.

IF YOU HAVE SEVERE SYMPTOMS

If you are experiencing severe symptoms, you need to get professional help. If you don't, you can expect chronic, if not permanent, disability. In the midst of feeling very distressed you may doubt you can recover fully. It is important for you to remind yourself that recovery is a process, not an event. You need to be patient with the process and trust that you will find your way back to health.

GETTING PROFESSIONAL HELP

In basic terms, a therapist is a well-educated, experienced, active listener. The therapist is there to serve you and be a facilitator in your healing process. A therapist's experience and training will help clarify what is going on inside you and help you learn to acknowledge your feelings.

Different educational pathways, training programs, and licensing requirements lead to different professional titles. For example, Marriage and Family Counselors, Psychotherapists, Psychologists, and Psychiatrists are among the more traditional therapists. And among the various professional groups, each individual practitioner has his/her own conceptual approach to therapeutic practice. Whatever their approach you need listening time and careful, honest feedback from a trained and experienced clinician.

The goal is to cleanse your wounds in a non-judgemental, supportive, and validating environment. If you do not feel rapport with the therapist, find someone else because the healing process will be compromised.

This does not mean you will always feel comfortable in the therapeutic process. The therapist may ask questions that challenge your views and bring up topics that might be disturbing, but you should have enough trust in the therapist and the therapeutic relationship to share the emotional intimacy.

To find a therapist ask your physician, attorney, religious leader, friends, or anyone whose opinion you trust for recommendations. If you do not feel comfortable asking someone you know, most metropolitan areas have crisis centers or psychotherapy referral networks. The phone book is usually a good starting point. The local chapter of MADD (Mothers Against Drunk Driving) is a good resource. Call the local District Attorney's office that has a Victim-Witness Assistance Program. This program often has a network of mental health professionals who specialize in treating trauma victims. United Way usually has a help line. A rape crisis center is also a good source of trauma specialists.

Ideally, you should locate a counselor who specializes in the treatment of car accident or trauma victims (rape, violent crime, natural disasters, sexual abuse, etc.) and has experience treating post-traumatic stress disorder. Unfortunately, a person with this background may be difficult to find in some areas.

Ask questions and shop around. When you first see a counselor, ask about his/her training and background. Consider what preference you have concerning the therapist's gender, age, and ethnic background. Also ask how many accident victims the therapist has worked with and how he/she conceptualizes the psychological healing process. You should be able to understand the therapist's explanation and feel good about his/her ability to communicate with you.

Do not feel afraid to speak with as many people as it takes to be satisfied. Finding a sensitive, experienced therapist with whom you feel compatible may take some time and a few phone calls. Trust your instincts but make sure you evaluate carefully because the therapist's opinions, values, and input can have an considerable influence on your recovery process.

DEALING WITH THE EMOTIONAL CHARGE OF THE RECOVERY PROCESS

In addition to the emotional impact of the accident trauma itself, the ongoing stress of dealing with the physical and economic repercussions of the accident create even more emotional dynamite. The surplus stress can undermine your productivity at work and cause conflict in your personal relationships. At times, your well of patience and energy may be near dry, but recognize that it is the fallout of the accident that is the source of the tension.

For example, physical injuries compromise your normal lifestyle. Depending on the extent of your injuries, the impact can be significant and long lasting. Injuries can introduce a lot of additional tension in your life; your sex life may be hampered, your kids expect you to be physically active with them but you can't, you can't exercise, just carrying the groceries or cleaning the house may be painful, and it may be hard just to sit in a chair at work. Changing your lifestyle to suit your physical limitations can be an emotional drain.

If you have soft tissue injuries it can be an especially confusing and frustrating time. To the outside world you look normal, but inside you are uncomfortable. Everyone expects you to be your usual self but you can't, at least not without finding new meaning for the word "pain." So you either try to ignore your discomfort, which causes more frustration and irritation, or you find yourself continually explaining to everyone how bad you feel, even though you look fine. It can be exhausting and emotionally taxing.

You need time to get proper medical attention. Even though your physical health is dependent on it, making the time for weekly visits to the physical therapist, the chiropractor, and the doctor can be exasperating. Medical visits can affect your work performance, work and home schedules, and your own patience.

Regardless of your physical health, you also have to deal with the economic consequences of the accident. Even in the best of situations—when all parties have adequate insurance and are cooperative—there will be phone calls and waiting, letters and waiting, claims paperwork and waiting, persistence and more waiting to finally reach an economic settlement. In the tougher cases, where fault might be at issue, or when you meet up with an insurance company or an attorney who is exceptionally demanding, you can become very frustrated. At its worst, the process can render meaningless characteristics like patience, respect, and compassion. Even with a healthy perspective on the whole affair, this aspect of your healing can add tremendous emotional tension to your life.

Finally, you might have to take time away from work, possibly without pay, to tend to your body, your automobile, your emotional health, and to deal with insurance issues. This may add money worries to the accident-tension stew.

Strain, whether physical, financial, emotional, or some combination, can surface and create unpleasant fireworks in personal relationships. In a sense, the accident touches more than just the individual(s) in the car. Everyone you interact with can feel the effects of the accident, particularly those closest to you.

The best way to survive this process, for yourself and those around you, is to make space for the accumulated tension. In a way, it is like an unwelcome relative who has come for a visit. Tension speaks with short-tempered anger, exhaustion, panic, depression, and in general, creates uneasy distance in relationships with others. There is no way to ignore it, so you acknowledge its presence and carefully adjust your life to the new pressures and limitations.

One of the ways to make this adjustment is to clearly communicate what you are feeling and what you need. The people around you, even those that love you, cannot read your mind. They may know you are uncomfortable, stressed, and frustrated with your healing process, but they cannot know "what you need" unless you communicate. The more you can openly share how you feel, the better they can understand how to be helpful and stay your allies in the healing process.

Mark

Emotionally, I had a difficult time after my accident. Every few nights I had violent nightmares and my stomach was upset for weeks. I also strained my lower back in the accident but after six weeks of treatment it didn't seem to be getting better.

I never really talked about the accident, or explained how I was feeling to my family. After a couple weeks, my family seemed to forget it happened. In their minds it was ancient history. But I was still in pain, both physically and emotionally. I was tense and impatient all the time, so at home everyone learned to just stay out of my way.

After I explained to my attorney how terrible I was feeling, he suggested that I see a professional therapist. After a couple sessions, the psychologist had me bring my whole family in. She helped me explain to them how dramatically I was still impacted by the accident. We all learned more effective ways to talk to one another and how they could support me through the healing process.

Even if you are not experiencing any of the symptoms of emotional trauma, you need and deserve to have your feelings of frustration and anger validated and supported. Sharing your feelings is a form of healing. Your family, friends, co-workers, and other significant people in your environment (doctors, lawyers, etc.) can influence your response to and recovery from the trauma. Their continued support and understanding can have a dramatic impact in helping you come to terms with your emotional discord. Take advantage of their support by including them and by keeping them informed and connected to all that is happening with you.

Although many will be supportive, you will not find the kind of compassion you deserve from everyone you come in contact with. Some friends or family members will be better than others at listening and supporting you. Use some discretion in evaluating the people and setting in which you confide your feelings.

If you find that you do not have anyone to share your experience with, your spouse seems tired of listening, and you are not getting the attention you want and need from your physician or attorney, see a professional counselor. It is not healthy to hold onto and internalize the frustration and anger you will sometimes feel in the course of the recovery process.

When your life becomes too stressful, it helps to simplify it. It may be hard, but take time to relax and do some enjoyable things. See an entertaining movie or video, take a walk somewhere pleasant, treat yourself to a nice dinner, or do whatever else makes you feel good. If you can arrange it, take a few mental health days off from work. Above all, treat yourself kindly and remember, all the issues related to the accident get taken care of eventually.

YOUR ACCIDENT NOTEBOOK

Remember to make entries in your accident notebook about your emotional well-being. Not only is this important for your economic settlement, but it can be a wonderful way of processing your feelings. You might find that a daily paragraph on how you are feeling is almost as satisfying as a talk with a friend. Indeed, your accident notebook is your friend through this period.

Don't worry about your grammar, no one will grade you. You don't have to write in complete sentences. Be as expressive and free as you want. The entries about your emotional state are for your eyes only unless you choose to share them. It is a private way for you to reflect on your feelings.

CHILDREN AND AUTOMOBILE ACCIDENTS

The information on psychological trauma in this and the previous chapter is equally valid and applicable to children. Children do not have an invisible deflector shield that protects them from experiencing fear and emotional trauma. The same events that cause psychological injury in adults can take an equal toll on children. In some cases, children are at a greater risk because they naturally experience the world with some degree of helplessness since they are dependent on their parents for survival. In fact, children are extremely sensitive to events in their environment, particularly those that impact their parent's well-being. This cannot be over-emphasized.

If your child has been involved in an automobile accident take special care to watch for signs of emotional discomfort. Similar to adults, their discomfort will show itself in both physical and emotional symptoms. Added difficulty arises because children are not as articulate in expressing what is going on inside themselves. Be attentive and provide a safe, supportive atmosphere so the child can express his/her uneasiness. Recognize that many feelings will be expressed and processed through play. Allow children to reinact the trauma using toys and dolls as often as necessary but don't hesitate to seek professional help from a child psychologist if you have questions or concerns. Although children are sensitive, they are physically and emotionally capable of full recovery given the proper attention.

If you have children and you have been in an accident, your children will be concerned. Because they care for you and are dependent on you for their well-being, it scares them when you are hurt in any way. Explain to them as often as necessary what you are experiencing and feeling and reassure them that you are doing all that is needed to make sure you get well. You will need to reassure them often, especially if you are physically or emotionally disabled by the accident.

Whether your children were in an accident or are just concerned for you, pretending that nothing is wrong will not help them. Again, denial is unhealthy. Children know when their parents are upset even if the parents pretend otherwise. Honest talk is the best policy. In the same way that an accident can lead to healthy changes for an adult, it can also teach a child crisis management skills which is an important part of emotional maturity.

IF THE ACCIDENT WAS YOUR FAULT

The vast majority of accidents are caused by inattentive or negligent drivers or drivers under the influence of alcohol or other drugs. Few accidents are intentionally caused. The fact is, humans make mistakes. Unfortunately, making a mistake with a motor vehicle can cause tremendous personal and property damage.

Most people responsible for an accident feel a sense of guilt, remorse, and regret. Accepting that your negligence seriously injured someone or perhaps caused a death is difficult and painful at best. The compassionate and healing thing to do is to apologize and communicate your sorrow. In most situations an authentic apology has tremendous healing power. Unfortunately, proper legal strategy does not coincide with the best emotional response. Most lawyers and insurers will tell you not to admit fault or make apologies until your legal case is complete. This doesn't help your conscience, or the people who were impacted by the accident.

Of course, only you can decide how to handle your responsibility for the accident. But at some point it is suggested that you communicate an apology. One option, if appropriate, is to write a letter of apology soon after the accident and hold onto it. Once you have approval from your attorney or insurer, mail it to the other party. Otherwise, you can wait until the legal aspect of the economic settlement is complete and then contact the other party in a way that feels comfortable to you.

It is important to recognize that economic recovery is separate from emotional recovery. Each has its own rules and timing, but one does not preclude the other. If it is economically necessary for you to bite your tongue for a time, then do so. But at some point it is respectful and healing, for everyone involved, to accept responsibility for your actions and to communicate that acknowledgement to those effected.

WHEN SOMEONE CLOSE TO YOU DIES IN THE ACCIDENT

Nothing can prepare you for the sudden, unexpected death of someone you love. This kind of personal loss can disrupt your life unlike any other. Your grief, anger, sadness, and confusion can take some time to work through.

At first, you might have a tremendous problem accepting the finality of the loss. You might find yourself in a state of numbed shock. Give yourself as much time as you need to digest the situation.

Slowly you will move through the denial and numbness, and start to feel the full force of your loss. Whether it was your spouse, child, or another family member, your world has shifted dramatically. You might feel terribly vulnerable, alone, and out of control.

You might also struggle with your anger; anger at the untimeliness of the death, its senselessness, and rage at the person responsible. Know that your feelings are okay. Anger is a normal response to such circumstances. Like all your other feelings, it is vital that you acknowledge your anger rather than hold it in. Behind your anger, fueling your anger, is sadness and hurt.

This kind of trauma can also show its impact in physical symptoms. The emotional turmoil can cause nightmares or troubled sleep, loss of appetite, stomach problems or headaches or other generalized physical pain, lack of energy, and general depression.

Above all, it will take time for you to deal with the loss. Inevitably, there will be tough times and later some times of relief. Allow your pain to surface. Just as dealing with other aspects of the accident trauma, you need to acknowledge your feelings, let them be real and expressed. Little by little you'll learn to adjust to the new reality.

You also need to monitor your physical symptoms. If your sleep is disrupted for any length of time, or any other unexplained physical symptoms persist, you should consider seeing a mental health professional. Of course, you don't have to wait for extreme symptoms before getting professional care.

There is a wide variety of resources available to help you work through your grief. One of the best books is *No Time For Goodbyes*, by Janice Harris Lord. Many other books are available on recovering from the loss of a loved one, as well as a number of organized support groups.

Please see the Resource section for some of the groups that can help you.

ALCOHOL-RELATED CRASHES

Sad but true, drunk driving is the most frequently committed crime in the United States. As previously stated, of the 40,000 killed in 1992 in auto crashes, nearly one half or 19,000 were killed in alcohol-related crashes. Alcohol is involved in about 10 percent of all wrecks. The more severe the accident, the more likely alcohol was involved. The fact is, drunk driving is the cause of tremendous personal devastation across our country.

If a drunk driver was the cause of your crash, in addition to all the other issues you face, you are undoubtedly enraged at the other driver. You may even fantasize about getting even and hurting the other driver. Again, your feelings are appropriate and okay. Certainly, you shouldn't act on these fantasies, but the anger that is fueling them is expected and appropriate.

Most important for you is to find a way to deal with your anger in a healthy manner. Bottled up inside you, it is literally like poison. As suggested in this chapter, the best thing to do is to find a safe, supportive environment to express your anger and hurt. Whether it is with friends, family, a support group, a professional therapist, through the court system, or all of the above, do not let your anger fester inside you.

If you want to stay actively involved with the criminal prosecution of the drunk driver, or just want to talk to people who specialize in this area, your local MADD chapter is an essential resource. Your local District Attorney's office may also have a Victim's Assistance Program. All states have adopted Victim's Rights statutes, each with varying provisions for financial, legal, and other assistance. Each Victim's Assistance Program office offers various services, depending on their resources.

On the other hand, if you drink and drive, or worse, if your drinking resulted in an crash, please get yourself educated. There is no acceptable reason to operate a vehicle when your driving ability is impaired. The risk is too great. If you are ready to look at your behavior, and indeed you may be forced to through a court sponsored education program, there are various resources available. In almost every metropolitan area there are alcohol and drug abuse support groups like Alcoholics Anonymous. Every bookstore has shelves and shelves of books on related topics. Most of all, you must be willing to explore your own life and make changes before these resources will help.

CONCLUSION

Unfortunately, "getting over the accident" can take a long time, especially considering the length of time it takes to obtain an economic settlement and legal closure. It may be incorrect to suggest that you will "get over it." You may continue to feel an uncomfortable twinge when you drive by the location of the accident. Your physical scars will remain as a reminder of the experience.

Nevertheless, whether it is the debilitating symptoms of post-traumatic stress disorder, the death of a spouse or family member, or any of the other psychological wounds that can result from a vehicle accident, dealing with the emotional turmoil is a doorway to change. As with your economic and physical recovery, it's important that you take responsibility for your emotional recovery by actively participating in the healing process. Shifting out of the frame of feeling victimized by the accident experience can be difficult. Undoubtedly, you wish it would fast become last week's news. But wholesome recovery does not occur, especially when emotional trauma is at issue, without your spirited and self-assertive participation.

Learning to do all this for yourself is a tremendous accomplishment. It is an opportunity for you to become stronger and more self-confident. The healing process can foster individual growth. In responding to the accident experience you learn more effective ways of looking inside yourself and taking responsibility for how you feel. Making healthy choices along the way may lead to a more wholesome life. Once you get perspective on the experience you will find that you have developed a more satisfying inner trust and strength. Given the enormous impact of the experience, personal values are not likely to remain unexamined or unaltered, and the change and growth bring added value and fullness to your life.

Important points to consider:

- The grieving process, telling your story from your heart, is the most direct pathway to emotional healing.
- If you are only mildly upset over the accident, talk to your spouse, a friend, or other confidant about how you feel, but do not ignore your feelings.
- If you are experiencing more than mild symptoms of emotional injury, consider seeking professional help.
- Do not hesitate to see a mental health professional if you are severely distraught over the accident.
- In general, picking up the pieces after an accident can be stressful. Be kind to yourself and allow room in your life for the extra stress.
- Record your emotional recovery process in your accident notebook.
- Children can be hurt emotionally as easily as adults. They need to be continually reassured if you are hurting. If they show signs of distress, do not hesitate to get them professional attention.
- Recovery is a process, not an event. Be patient and trust in your ability to heal.

Chapter 7

A PRELUDE TO ECONOMIC HEALING

THE INSURANCE POLICY MAZE

When you buy your automobile insurance policy, you are paying your insurance company (also called your "insurer") to assume a limited monetary risk over any accident in which you are involved. The company can afford this type of economic roulette because it has millions of premium paying policyholders, only a small fraction of whom will be involved in accidents.

You, understandably, make this deal with the insurance company because the risk of going uninsured is too great. The hardship of an accident without insurance protection would be economically devastating which is why many states legally require at least minimum coverage.

Most insurance companies try to hedge the odds in their favor by screening their customers, accepting only good drivers, or charging young or high risk drivers higher premiums. They then try to maximize their profits by wisely investing your premium dollars and carefully scrutinizing policy claims before paying out any money.

Overall, the insurance industry is immense. With over 6,000 companies in the United States alone, they receive more than $400 billion per year in premiums. Insurance companies, like banks, car manufacturers, and the corner grocer are in business to make a profit. They are interested in their economic health, just as you are. The less they pay out on policy claims, the more their premium dollars are available for investment, and the larger the "P" in the company's profit.

This is not meant as a criticism of the industry, but just a statement of fact. Whether it is with your own insurer or another driver's, it is important that you keep the profit motive perspective in mind when making an insurance claim. If you expect the claims adjuster to rush to your aching side with a blank "Big Bank" check, you will likely be disappointed and empty handed. But neither should you expect to be stonewalled or denied fair compensation based on your contractual and legal rights.

Rather, what you should expect is that you will have to justify your economic claim and sometimes aggressively pursue it until you are satisfied. Undoubtedly, the last thing you might feel capable of doing is wade through the bewildering legal mire of insurance policies and the claims process. A wonderful world it would be if you could go off to some tropical island and heal your wounds while the insurance company repairs the financial wounds associated with your accident. Sorry to say, that is not the way the system operates.

Since it's unlikely you can afford the economic burden of a long and expensive recovery process without an insurance settlement, stepping into the mire, to the extent necessary to ensure a healthy economic recovery, is unavoidable. So jump into your hip waders and swampboots, and prepare for your journey to economic health.

FAULT VS. NO-FAULT LEGAL / INSURANCE SYSTEMS

Although the specific rules in each state vary, there are only two basic legal frameworks — fault and no-fault — that control who pays (in legalese this is called "economic liability") for damages resulting from automobile accidents. On the one hand, the fault system requires that "fault" be determined through an investigation by the insurance companies involved and/or by a court judgment before economic responsibility is apportioned. Normally, whomever is legally at fault pays for the damages.

On the other hand, in theory the no-fault system is designed to simplify this process by providing every accident victim with immediate compensation, regardless of who is to blame. Since both systems are in operation throughout the country, and some states even have a blend of both, we need to address the ins and outs of each.

WHEN FAULT IS AT ISSUE

The concept of fault is fairly simple; through mistake or otherwise, someone or something is usually to blame for every automobile accident. The legal issue in determining fault in most accidents is deciding whose negligent driving caused the accident. The basic premise of the fault system is that the person or people whose negligence caused the accident are legally responsible (insurance companies and lawyers use the term "liable") for the resulting damages.

In the early stages of the claims process, it is usually the insurance claims adjuster or representative (claims rep) who tries to determine who is at fault (and thus liable for damages) based on the police report, the statements of those involved in the accident, and witnesses to the accident. If the claims adjuster(s) cannot settle the fault issue, or as in some cases, if lawyers are involved at the onset, the attorneys for each side continue with more detailed investigations and negotiations to determine fault and thus who will be liable for damages. Ultimately, if the attorneys cannot settle on who is legally responsible and for how much, a judge and/or a jury makes the determination as the result of a formal lawsuit.

The legal concept of fault is a bit more complicated than that used on the playground and to make matters worse, each state has its own detailed standards for fault and for calculating the monetary liability resulting from auto accidents. These individual nuances can be very important because monetary and legal responsibility are at issue, but most of the grueling details are only interesting to and necessary for lawyers and claims adjusters.

However, there is an important twist to the legal concept of fault that you should be familiar with. In the fault system, economic responsibility for damage costs rest on the person who caused the accident. But sometimes both drivers' negligence contributes, in varying degrees, to the accident and thus fault is not clear-cut. In these situations, the goal is to divide or apportion damage costs according to the degree of fault. As you can imagine, this is not necessarily an easy task, especially when a good deal of money is at stake. In complicated cases, when lawyers and insurance companies point their fingers in blame, depending on which state they are in, they use the terms contributory and comparative negligence.

Comparative negligence. Most states use the rule of comparative negligence in apportioning damages. Under this system, your damage claim is reduced by the amount you are found to be at fault. For example, if your actions were found to contribute 40% to the cause of the accident, then you would only be entitled to 60% of your full damage claim. The variations on this rule are many, but most importantly, in some states, if you are greater than 50% at fault you cannot recover against another driver's liability coverage at all.

Contributory negligence. The old and somewhat brutal contributory negligence rules are still followed in some states. Under this system, if your negligent actions contributed to the accident in any way, even minimally, you cannot recover damages under another driver's liability coverage.

HOW DAMAGE COMPENSATION IS DETERMINED

Once the determination of who is liable for damages is made, the issue of fair and reasonable compensation is then addressed. When lawyers, insurance companies, and courts consider the damages resulting from an accident, they group them into three legal classifications: special damages, general damages, and punitive damages.

Special damages. The tangible, substantiated out-of-pocket expenses that you incur when recovering from the accident are called special damages. They include medical bills, rehabilitation costs, lost wages, property damage, and car rental. Depending on the injuries and the property damage, special damages can add up to a significant amount of money. Imagine the mounting medical expense and lost wages while healing from a broken leg and internal injuries. The total cost could easily approach $50,000 to $100,000 within a few months.

General damages. The major controversy over personal injury lawsuits and the fault system concerns the size of general damage awards. Unlike the concrete value of special damages, general damages are those costs that cannot be given an objective value, but are nonetheless quite real and substantial. They refer to the emotional pain and suffering, and the temporary or permanent physical and psychological compromises that the accident might force into your life.

What is fair compensation for the loss of a spouse, or an amputated arm, or facial disfigurement, or eighteen months of painful rehabilitation following a serious whiplash, or the despair of post-traumatic stress disorder, or thirty years of chronic back pain? A million dollars, a thousand, or perhaps nothing? These are the questions confronting insurance companies, attorneys, accident victims, and courts every day. To make matters more complicated and seemingly arbitrary, general damage awards vary from state to state and jury to jury. As a very rough estimate, insurance companies and attorneys figure general damages to fall between 1 to 5 times the total medical billing.

Punitive damages. Although rarely an issue in automobile accident cases, punitive damages are most often assessed against an insurance company if it violates its legal duty to treat you and your claim in "good faith." Punitive damages are a form of economic penalty meant to punish and deter unfair or "bad faith" conduct. For example, many bad faith punitive damage awards occur when an insurance company unjustifiably refuses to pay a valid claim, fails to investigate a claim adequately, or unreasonably delays claims processing.

Establishing proof of bad faith can be difficult because insurers are allowed to scrutinize claims rigorously before deciding whether payment is justified. There exists an array of questionable tactics which do not fall under the legal definition of bad faith. As a result, proving the company acted in bad faith usually requires a flagrant wrongdoing.

Paul

Paul was driving out of a supermarket parking lot. As he was completing a left turn onto a busy road another vehicle crashed into the front passenger side of his car. After an investigation, the insurance companies involved agreed that the other driver was 90% at fault and Paul was 10% to blame for the accident. Paul lives in a state which follows the comparative fault rules.

Paul suffered a broken arm and a whiplash. He was unable to work for almost two months and was in a rehabilitation program for almost six months. Paul was reimbursed by his own company for car repairs, less his deductible. His settlement with the other driver's insurer was not finalized until nine months after the accident. The final settlement was as follows:

Medical Bills (numerous sources)	$8,500
Wage losses	$3,000
Car rental	$300
Collision deductible	$500
General damages (2X medical bills)	$17,000
Total	$29,300
less 10% comparative fault	-$2,930
Settlement	$26,370
Attorney's fees (33%)	-$8,702
Paul receives	$17,668

DOES THE FAULT SYSTEM WORK?

Overall, the fault system does not have many admirers. Criticisms have been voiced from consumers' groups, personal injury attorneys, and the insurance industry. Most everyone agrees that the fault system keeps many personal injury attorneys very busy and well paid, while auto insurance rates are too high and the claims process is too time-consuming and rough on you, the accident victim. For example, if you were involved in a difficult case that took years to settle, it would put a cruel and unnecessary economic burden on your life.

Moreover, fault determination can be complicated by dishonest, uncooperative, and greedy people whose words and intentions become even more muddled by the elaborate insurance/legal framework. The idiosyncrasies and egos of the people involved can confound the legal process even more.

Finally, spreading blame for some accidents may be a very arbitrary process. And just because you might mistakenly cause an accident—with over 34 million accidents a year, one has to conclude that normally responsible, upstanding people do cause accidents—how severe should the lasting consequences be? The "no-fault" system is supposed to do away with many of the problems of the fault system.

THE NO-FAULT SYSTEM

No-fault insurance is designed so that you receive damage compensation from your own insurance company regardless of who is to blame. Compensation is limited by your particular insurance coverage and the laws of the individual state. In a no-fault system, you no longer have to wade through months of frustrating negotiations and possibly a lawsuit to recoup the economic costs of an accident from an at-fault driver. If you are involved in an accident, you need only deal with your own insurer to recover medical care costs, lost wages, and other out of pocket expenses (special damages). Hence the name "no-fault," because regardless of who caused the accident insurance companies are only responsible to their own clients.

To make the insurance affordable for both the insurance industry and the consumer, the theoretical no-fault system severely restricts the right to sue. A claim must reach a certain threshold of severity (either large monetary damages or severe injuries) before a lawsuit is allowed. Under monetary threshold rules a lawsuit is permitted if recovery costs exceed a certain dollar value — for example, in Connecticut the monetary threshold is $400. If that seems to defeat the purpose of no-fault, you are right. Read on and we'll explain. Verbal thresholds describe the nature of injuries that must be sustained before a lawsuit is allowed. A verbal threshold might require that someone suffer permanent disfigurement or impairment of bodily function. With these restrictions in effect, costly lawsuits and inflated general damage (pain and suffering) awards are oftentimes avoided. The money saved by forgoing fault determination, expensive law suits, and limiting compensation to special damages lowers premiums and can also allow for more comprehensive benefit packages.

Michigan, for example, has perhaps the most successful no-fault system in the country. The mandatory no-fault coverage there requires insurance policies to provide unlimited medical and rehabilitation benefits, up to approximately $100,000 for lost income (an injured person can receive 80% of gross income up to the 1992 maximum of about $2600 a month for a limited period), survivors benefits, and limited reimbursement for some substitution services. Michigan no-fault coverage also pays up to $1 million for damage to other people's property, but policyholders must purchase separate collision coverage (see discussion below) to cover damage to their own vehicles and property damage liability coverage for protection when driving outside the state.

Balancing the generous benefits, the flip-side of Michigan no-fault law establishes tough restrictions on the right to sue. Generally, fault determining lawsuits are allowed if a victim "dies, suffers permanent and serious disfigurement, or serious impairment of bodily function." Only in these limited cases can accident victims recover general damages for pain and suffering and the like, and only if they are successful in their lawsuits.

For some accident victims, no-fault coverage means the difference between wholesome recovery and complete economic ruin.

Nick

> *Nick was paralyzed from the waist down when he crashed his motorcycle head-on into an automobile on a Michigan highway. Nick had been racing his motorcycle and was apparently largely to blame for the accident. In addition to losing the use of his legs, Nick crushed three vertebrae, fractured an arm, and suffered internal injuries.*
>
> *Needless to say, he spent several months in the hospital and his rehabilitation program continues to this day. Under Michigan's no-fault law, Nick's insurance covered all medical and rehabilitation expenses not paid by his health insurance. The total bill was well over $100,000.*
>
> *If the accident had occurred in a fault determining state, Nick would have had to rely on his automobile insurance medical coverage (commonly people have coverage limits of $10,000 or less) and his health insurance (which normally covers only 80% of medical costs and very little if any rehabilitation expenses). In addition, Nick would not have been able to make a claim against the other driver's liability coverage because he was at fault. No doubt, the no-fault coverage saved Nick from bankruptcy and ensured his continued recovery.*

The Michigan system benefits its insured drivers in almost every situation, as the example above suggests. The Auto Club Insurance Association found that in Michigan in 1986, it paid about 73 cents of every premium dollar to accident victims compared to only 48 cents to accident victims in fault determining states. It also found that only 4 cents of every dollar was spent on court costs and attorney fees in Michigan, while in other states, 32 cents of every dollar went to those same expenses. While no-fault has, in theory, many advantages over the fault system, in practice, Michigan has just about the only successful no-fault system in the country.

Unfortunately, just about every other state that has incorporated some aspects of a no-fault system has done it poorly. All state laws are products of political compromise between trial lawyers (who stand to lose the most from a true no-fault system), insurance companies, and consumers' groups. Almost all the states that have some form of no-fault insurance in operation (about 15 states), have watered-down, ineffective systems. In most of these states, the no-fault concept was simply added into the existing fault system. This type of blended no-fault/fault product is a confusing mess. Most no-fault systems in the country are not keeping insurance companies or consumers happy.

Some of the significant problems with current no-fault laws include:

- **Lawsuits are still a concern**. Many state no-fault laws provide a reasonable special damage benefit package but do not balance it with restrictions on lawsuits. So, if an accident causes more than a relatively minor dollar value threshold (remember Connecticut's $400 threshold) victims may still sue one another. As a result, lawsuits have not declined, insurance premiums have still sky-rocketed, and consumers must pay for both liability insurance and no-fault.

- **Property damage is often still a "fault" issue**. In many no-fault states, liability for property damage is still determined by who is at fault. Consumers must still pay for property damage liability coverage to protect themselves against a lawsuit and may have to sue to recover for their own property damage. This is even more troublesome because most lawyers will only work on a contingency basis, taking a percentage of the damage award, if the value of the case is enough to entice them. Otherwise the victim must pay the attorney an hourly fee. On this basis, attorney's fees might end up costing as much as the value of the damages.

- **No compensation for general damages**. Most no-fault systems prevent victims from receiving compensation for pain and suffering and other general damages, unless the no-fault laws allow them to sue. Thus, even if you suffer chronic pain as a result of the accident, in some no-fault states you may not be able to receive compensation.

- **Inadequate compensation for special damages**. Many no-fault systems do not have the realistic benefit packages that exist in Michigan. Michigan limits the amount of lost-wage recovery, regardless of the circumstances. The no-fault medical and lost wage benefit provisions may be so inadequate that all those who are permitted by law to sue will do so to get adequate compensation.

As with most things in life, there is no clear answer to the problems of the fault and the no-fault systems. Since we will continue to drive cars, there will be accident trauma victims who can never really be adequately compensated regardless of the method or the price. As an accident victim, your economic health is dependent on the system in which you live. As a consumer of legal services and an insurance premium payer it is worth your time to be educated and voice your opinion.

YOUR INSURANCE POLICY

Most automobile insurance policies, whether in a fault or no-fault state, are really a combination of several different types of coverages grouped into a single policy package. Some portions of the policy are designed to pay you, the insured, when you are injured and/or your property is damaged by an automobile accident, regardless of fault. Other portions of the policy are meant to protect you legally and economically from the other people involved in the accident. Each state has legal requirements making some types of coverage mandatory and others optional. Each coverage item has its separate price, the sum being the premium you pay each year.

LIABILITY COVERAGE

Two types of coverage—bodily injury coverage and property damage coverage—are meant to insulate you from economic claims made by other people in the accident. Together, these two types of coverage are called *liability* protection because the insurance company agrees, up to the limits of your individual policy, to assume economic responsibility (liability) for the damage *you cause to others* as a result of the accident. Under liability coverage, the insurance company is only obligated to pay up to the limits specified in your policy. If the damage you cause exceeds your policy limits, the balance comes out of your pocket. Therefore, it is important to consider the amount of coverage you realistically need to protect your assets if you are found legally responsible for the damages caused by an accident.

In fault states, liability coverage (or a bond equivalent) is the only legally required automobile insurance. In no-fault states, no-fault coverage (see "personal injury protection" below) is compulsory in addition to liability coverage.

BODILY INJURY LIABILITY COVERAGE

Bodily injury coverage applies when other people are injured by your automobile and you are found at fault. This portion of your insurance policy is meant to protect you from bearing the economic burden of other people's injuries. This coverage applies only when it is determined, by investigation or a court judgment, that you are legally liable for all or some portion of the accident damages.

Under this coverage, the insurance company will compensate pedestrians, or people riding in other cars *for the injuries you caused.* Bodily injury liability coverage pays for most special and general damages including medical bills, lost wages, and compensation for pain and suffering or disabilities resulting from the accident.

When you purchase bodily injury coverage, you choose how much liability protection you want. The policy limits you purchase are expressed in either a *single-limit* or *split-limit* amount. In a split-limit policy, the insurance company agrees to pay a maximum amount *per injured person* and *per accident for all injured people.* For example, California requires that each person insuring a motor vehicle has a minimum bodily injury coverage of $15,000 per injured person and $30,000 per accident.

Single-limit coverage limits the total amount the insurance company will pay per accident but not the per person amount. The distinction between the two types of bodily injury coverage can be important.

PROPERTY DAMAGE LIABILITY COVERAGE

The **property damage** portion of liability coverage only applies to other people's property damaged by your automobile. Under property damage liability coverage, if you are found to be legally responsible, the insurance company will compensate *other people* for the damage caused to their property by the accident. Usually the damage is to another vehicle, but it includes anything of value. Over half of insurance company payments are for property damage claims.

Like bodily injury coverage, you purchase a specified maximum property damage coverage as a part of your automobile insurance policy. California, for example, requires a $5,000 minimum property damage coverage for all drivers. Considering the value of cars today, $5,000 of coverage only pays for a small portion of most new cars. In a 1991 article, *Consumer Reports* recommended that people purchase, at a minimum, $25,000 in property damage coverage.

LIABILITY COVERAGE AND THE COST OF A LAWSUIT

The final aspect of the liability protection you purchase from the insurance company is the cost they incur defending you against a lawsuit. You don't pay for this separately, but the cost is included in the price you pay for the liability coverage portions of your policy. It drives insurance premiums up but it can literally save you thousands of dollars. Imagine having to pay lawyers, expert witnesses (doctors, accident reconstruction specialists, private detectives, etc.) and all the other expenses vital to defending a lawsuit. The insurance company orchestrates and pays for all of this when it defends a claim brought against your policy for the bodily injury and property damage caused by an automobile accident for which you are to blame.

MEDICAL PAYMENTS (MedPay)

Medical payments coverage (called MedPay) provides for medical expenses incurred by you and the occupants of your insured car when involved in an accident, regardless of fault. MedPay also pays medical expenses for you and others eligible in your household, if injured in someone else's car or as a pedestrian. This coverage pays for medical expenses only, not lost wages or general damages (pain and suffering or disabilities). Your MedPay coverage has a specified maximum dollar limit and will only cover expenses for a specific period of time following the accident.

If, after receiving MedPay benefits, you recover damages which include medical costs from another party in the accident, most insurance policies require that you reimburse your insurer for its payments. In other words, you cannot collect double benefits.

Tom

I was walking across a busy street when a car ran a red light and hit me. I broke my collar bone and got a moderate concussion when I hit the pavement. Over the course of six months, my medical treatment and rehabilitation expenses were approximately $15,000, $10,000 of which was paid for by my MedPay coverage.

After nine months of negotiations, I settled with the driver's insurance company for a total of $50,000 as reimbursement for my medical expenses and pain and suffering, but $10,000 of that went directly to my insurer to repay the MedPay coverage I received.

MedPay is optional coverage and it might duplicate some aspects of a general health insurance policy you already have, but you should look closely at the details of each policy before forgoing MedPay coverage. Note: some health insurance policies do not require reimbursement if you later receive an insurance settlement, so it is worth your while to be familiar with the nuances of all your insurance coverages.

PERSONAL INJURY PROTECTION (PIP)

The no-fault equivalent of MedPay is called personal injury protection or PIP coverage. The difference is that PIP is often the legally required form of coverage for no-fault states and it is generally more comprehensive than MedPay. Depending on the laws of the particular state, it may cover lost wages and other replacement services in addition to medical expenses, regardless of fault. The maximum coverage, coverage term, and other policy limits of PIP are largely dependent on the no-fault legal mandates of each individual state.

PIP coverage is really the only unique aspect of insurance in a no-fault state. Otherwise, those insured under no-fault rules carry insurance coverage identical to those in fault states. For example, no-fault drivers need liability protection for fault accidents which might either occur while driving in another state or for those situations where a lawsuit is allowed in the no-fault state itself.

COLLISION AND COMPREHENSIVE COVERAGE

Collision coverage is an optional part of your insurance coverage. If your car is damaged from "physical impact with another vehicle" your insurance company pays to fix it (less your deductible), regardless of who is to blame for the accident, if you have collision coverage.

Comprehensive coverage is also optional. It works the same as collision, in that fault is not at issue, but it covers damage to your vehicle in situations "other than collision," such as fire, theft, storms, hitting an animal, etc.

Collision/comprehensive coverage pays for the amount of repair or the "actual cash value of the property," less a specified deductible. Together they can make up 25 to 50% of your annual premium and misunderstanding the limits of the collision/comprehensive coverage you pay for can also cause a great deal of frustration when the check arrives from the insurance company.

Betty

> *I was trying to make a left turn across a busy street and was struck by an oncoming car. The front and passenger side of my car was severely damaged. My car was relatively new, with about 20,000 miles on it, and in reasonably good shape.*

> *After inspecting the car, my insurance company's claims representative explained my entitlement under my collision coverage. He said that I would be reimbursed for only one-half the cost of a new paint job, since only half the car was damaged by the accident. In addition, he pro-rated the value of my two destroyed tires; since they had 20,000 miles on them, the company would only cover the value of the tires at the time they were destroyed.*

> *The repair job cost $3,100. Of that, $500 was for new paint and $300 for tires. But the insurer would only pay for 50% of the paint job, or $250 and only $150 for the tires. My deductible was $300, so I ended up paying $700, almost 25% of the repair costs to get my car back.*

Once you are paid for a claim on your collision or comprehensive coverage, your insurance company is then legally entitled to attempt to get reimbursement from the other driver or his insurer through a legal process called "subrogation." Your insurer may ask for your participation in their lawsuit. Alternatively, if, after receiving collision or comprehensive benefits, you collect a settlement which includes property damage expenses from another insurer, most insurance policies require that you reimburse your own insurance company for its payments. Like MedPay, you are usually not entitled to receive double payments for your damages.

UNINSURED MOTORIST

Uninsured motorist coverage (UMI) provides protection for medical bills, lost wages, and pain and suffering when you are injured by an at-fault but uninsured motorist. Without this coverage, if you are involved in an accident and the other driver is at fault but uninsured, you have to sue the other driver (if he/she has any personal assets) and/or rely on your MedPay to pay for all your health care costs (remember MedPay does not pay for pain and suffering or lost wages) and collision coverage to pay for your vehicle. When the other driver is at fault but uninsured, you do not have the option of making a claim against their liability coverage.

Most UMI policies only provide for bodily injury costs and not property damage. You have to purchase uninsured motorist property damage coverage (UMPD) separately to pay for damage to your property by an at-fault, uninsured driver, as an alternative or supplement to collision coverage.

UMI only comes into effect when the other driver was at fault but uninsured. It pays you what you would have been legally entitled to if the other driver had proper insurance, but it comes from your own insurance company. Hopefully, you and your insurance company reach some equitable settlement, but if you cannot agree, the case is referred to arbitration before going to court.

An important point to remember is that uninsured motorist coverage and MedPay work together. For example, if you have $20,000 worth of medical bills after being injured by an at-fault, uninsured driver and you have $10,000 MedPay coverage, your uninsured motorist coverage pays the other $10,000 and not the full $20,000 in addition to your MedPay. In other words, you cannot get double payment for your damages.

Some companies offer underinsured motorist coverage which is similar to uninsured motorist coverage for the situations where the other driver's insurance limits are inadequate to pay for the total amount of your damages. Other companies include this coverage in their uninsured motorist coverage.

INSURANCE COVERAGE SUMMARY

In general, you pay your insurance company to protect you in two different ways. First, your liability coverage (bodily injury and property damage) protects you from paying for damage that you cause someone else. With this coverage, if you are found legally responsible for the accident, the insurance company is obliged to pay up to the limits of your policy. Your liability coverage does not pay to heal your own injuries.

To receive compensation for your own bodily injuries you either need MedPay (fault system) or PIP coverage (no-fault system); and to repair your vehicle you need some form of comprehensive/collision coverage. If you have the appropriate coverage, you can file a claim on your own insurance policy, regardless of who is to blame for the accident. With these coverages, your insurance company is obligated to compensate you up to the limits of your policy.

Finally, you can also receive compensation by making a claim against the other driver's liability insurance coverage for your injuries, assuming of course that the other driver is primarily at fault (and the no-fault rules in your state allow this type of claim). In general, your insurance company is not involved in this aspect of your case; you only pay them to defend you against claims, not initiate claims on your behalf. When you make a claim against another insurance company, you either go it alone, or get a personal injury attorney to handle your claim for you.

CONCLUSION

It is absolutely vital to your recovery that you understand the privileges and limitations embodied in your insurance policy. This is especially true if you plan to pursue your insurance claim without an attorney. Take your time and reread the chapter if necessary (sorry, but it is that important). You can be certain that the opposing insurance company will have an intimate understanding of how to make its policies work to its economic benefit. If you need further clarification, your insurance agent, claims representative, or attorney should be able to answer any of your questions.

Here are some of the important points to remember:

- Insurance companies are interested in their own economic health, which means they will carefully exaimine your accident claim before paying you any money.

- In the fault system, the person at fault is legally responsible for the damages caused by the accident.

- In the no-fault system, some damages are compensated by each individual's insurance regardless of fault.

- Most no-fault systems allow fault-determining lawsuits in many situations.

- Your insurance policy is composed of several separate types of coverage, including: bodily injury and property damage liability coverage, medical payments coverage (MedPay), personal injury protection (PIP), comprehensive/collision coverage, and uninsured motorist coverage.

- Liability coverage protects you against claims made by other drivers if you are to blame for an accident.

When you make a claim on another driver's insurance policy, you make it against their liability coverage.

- MedPay covers your accident injuries regardless of fault.

- PIP is the no-fault equivalent of MedPay, and is usually more comprehensive in coverage.

- Collision/comprehensive coverage reimburses you for the damage to your vehicle, regardless of fault.

- Uninsured motorist coverage pays you if you are injured by an uninsured driver.

- There are three separate scenarios which compose the claims process: making a claim on your own insurance coverage, helping your insurer defend you against claims on your liability coverage, and making a claim against another driver's insurance policy.

NOTES

Chapter 8

ECONOMIC HEALING

FAIRNESS DEPENDS ON WHERE YOU SIT

Now that you have a general idea of the protection you buy when you pay your insurance policy premiums and the legal framework through which your economic recovery will proceed, you are ready to tackle the slippery slopes of the claims process. It is on these grades that you might feel most like Sisyphus pushing the boulder up a never-ending incline because economic recovery is usually much more complicated than making a single call to your insurance company and waiting for the check to arrive.

Notifying your own insurance company is usually the correct *first step*, but depending upon the circumstances, you will, in all likelihood, have more calls to make before your situation is resolved. There are a number of variables which determine how smoothly your claims process will proceed. These include: the types of insurance coverage you and the other driver have, the dollar value of damages, who is at fault and whether all parties involved agree on this determination, the length of time that physical and psychological treatment will be necessary, and whether the parties and the insurance companies are cooperating with one another. Be warned, working "the system:" interacting with claims representatives, attorneys, and the assorted other people involved in the recovery process, can cause considerable frustration and disappointment. The temptation is to let the boulder go and accept a less than equitable insurance settlement just to end the toil.

This chapter will demystify the claims process so that fighting for your economic health doesn't seem like such a struggle. With a clear understanding of how the system operates and what to expect, you can more effectively and responsibly help yourself reach a wholesome economic recovery.

THE CLAIMS PROCESS

Consumer Reports has consistently found that auto insurance companies handle claims to the complete satisfaction of consumers only 60 percent of the time. The most common complaints concern delays in handling claims, disagreements over the dollar amount of damages, conflicts over fault determination, and complaints about too much red tape.

Before you are convinced it is insurance companies that are to blame for all the flaws in the system, consider the nature of the insurance beast itself. The business relies on honest dealings between potential adversaries—consumers (and their attorneys) versus insurance companies (and their attorneys)—all of whom are trying to protect their economic interests.

The reported dissatisfaction results from a mix of unrealistic expectations, a lack of understanding of the process, and difficulties on the insurance company end. Whatever the cause, it seems you might run into problems at just about every step in the process.

Insurance companies do have good reason to be somewhat cautious and skeptical in examining claims against their policies. In addition to the immense legal and administrative costs of settling billions of dollars in legitimate claims, they must guard themselves against billions more in inflated or fraudulent claims. Some experts estimate that as much as 20 cents of every dollar paid out goes towards padded or fraudulent automobile claims. Not only accident victims, but also lawyers, medical professionals, auto repair shops, and even claims representatives are responsible for these schemes.

Unfortunately, as a result, it is the honest policyholders who must endure increased scrutiny of their claims. Because so much money is lost to illegitimate claims, there is less money available to pay justifiable ones. With so many people and so much money involved, and the system being so huge, it is a wonder that it functions at all.

In any event, the economic recovery process is based on settlement negotiations between you, the accident victim (and/or your legal representative), and the claims representative. How the system works for you on an individual basis is largely dependent both on your knowledge of the system and on the ability and attitude of the claims representative assigned to your particular case. Some claims representatives like the job, do it well, and take pride in their ability; others might seem to be doing everything they can to intensify your accident nightmare. Of course, the same could be said of all the professionals whose livelihoods depend on working with accident victims.

In general, most insurance company claims representatives (these are not the same people who sold you your policy) are overworked and underpaid. In addition, claims representatives are often judged more on how adeptly they limit the amount of dollars paid out on claims and much less on how conscientiously they take care of you, the accident victim.

Perhaps as important as the individual facts of the case and the substance of your claim, is the way you present your demands to the claims representative. This is true whether you are dealing with your own company or the other driver's. As one claims representative told us, "you get more with honey: courtesy, respect, and determined patience will go a lot further than busting in with both six-shooters drawn."

Even though you may be angry, impatient, in physical pain, worried about all the money it takes to get well, and wish someone would have mercy and take care of your mess, most claims representatives have files overflowing with cases similar to yours. They just do not have the time to patiently walk you through the process, nor can they get emotionally involved in each case. Your best bet is to make room elsewhere in your life to take care of the emotional impact of the accident and remain businesslike in your dealings with insurance companies.

Finally, do not file false claims or exaggerate your loss by overdramatizing your injuries. Both are illegal and amplify the costly, adversarial nature of the system. Padded claims make claims representatives more suspicious and demanding. Fraudulent claims raise the cost of doing business and thus come back to haunt you in increased premiums at best, at worst you may be charged with a crime. The temptation exists because it seems like free money, but chances are you won't fool anyone. You may get your money, but your claim will be heavily scrutinized. If you deal with an insurer in a straightforward, honest, manner, the company is legally obliged to treat you and your claim in a similar manner and will do so. If the company breaches its duty to process your claim in good faith, then you may be able to collect a hefty punitive damage penalty.

With the above as a preface, remember — in most cases it is a combination of knowing and doing the right things and having a healthy, realistic perspective tempered with patient determination, which will best facilitate your economic recovery. Honest, well-documented claims presented in a courteous fashion are more likely to get personalized treatment than impatient, condescending demands.

The central component of the claims process is really a combination of three separate scenarios: (1) working with your insurance company to defend claims brought against your liability coverage; (2) making a claim against your own insurance company and your own policy to pay for some portions of your own injuries; and (3) making a claim against the other driver's insurance policy. After a quick discussion about reporting an accident to your insurer and a few comments on properly documenting your claim, we will detail these three scenarios.

IF AND WHEN TO REPORT AN ACCIDENT

Regardless of who is to blame, or whether you are in a no-fault or fault system, the first thing you need to do after being involved in an accident, in almost all situations, is notify your insurance company. Even if the accident seems inconsequential at first, when everyone involved is apparently unharmed and agrees to settle the situation privately, you want to seriously consider including your insurance company. Your premiums pay for economic protection and there are very, very few accident situations where you can safely forego that security.

Most insurance policies require that an accident be reported "promptly." If you zip your lips and your insurer later finds out about the accident through routine checks of traffic records, the company might raise your premiums or refuse to renew your policy. The company can even refuse to pay claims stemming from an unreported accident. Imagine your shock if, a month or two after privately paying a few hundred dollars to the other driver whose fender you crunched, you get notice that the other driver is suing you for assorted physical injuries and pain and suffering. To make matters worse, the other driver's lawyer argues that since you initially paid for the damage to the vehicle you admitted fault and are therefore responsible for all remaining damages. If your company covers the claim, it may refuse to renew your policy because you have become a high risk driver.

Like most businesses, insurance companies are concerned about expensive surprises, especially the kind that can be prevented with proper warning. When you bring the insurer into the picture at the beginning, the company can investigate the accident while the facts are still fresh. Insurance companies want to be involved at the onset so they can use their expertise to avoid expensive lawsuits and minimize damage costs.

Admittedly, not every metal to metal bump and grind is lawsuit material. Insurance companies probably overdramatize the costs of unreported accidents and the threat of lawsuits. Some experts suggest that insurers can safely be left out if no one is injured in the accident and the damages are less than two hundred dollars. But, considering how slowly some soft tissue injuries develop, you want to carefully weigh the consequences of a minor accident that might get complicated later.

Unfortunately, if you are at fault for the accident, your premiums will probably be increased, sometimes by 30% or more. Although each company has its own guidelines, most raise premiums if you cause a "chargeable accident," usually one that costs the company more than a few hundred dollars. Other companies, however, are legally required to use the state's traffic-point system, only raising rates when you reach a point threshold based on traffic citations as well as accidents.

Most companies will, without much fuss, tell you how an accident will affect your premiums. If you are deciding whether you want to report a minor accident, you may even want to discuss the situation with a claims representative informally. Once you know your options, you can decide whether to file an official report.

Until the statue of limitations for filing a lawsuit has expired (it varies from state to state, but is usually one or two years), you are at risk, however slight it may be, of being sued, unless you have a legally enforceable claims release from the other driver. On the other hand, before you sign a release giving up your right to make a claim relating to an accident, give yourself and your body time to stabilize. In the end, the judgment is yours, but be careful about deciding to assume the full economic risk of an accident by excluding your insurance company.

DOCUMENTING YOUR CLAIM PUTS MONEY IN YOUR POCKET

Insurance companies and the legal system in general puts tremendous emphasis on the written word. When disputes arise, insurance companies and attorneys don't care much about what you think you bought when you paid your premiums, they look to the words printed in the policy to decide who owes whom. When you present your claim for $20,000 in medical expenses, you should have written records totaling that amount or you will not get the money. Or, if you have to sue your attorney for malpractice, your case will be much more salient and convincing if you have copies of letters of complaint documenting poor handling of the case over time, rather than hoping your verbal recollection of events will be compelling enough.

The more completely and meticulously you organize and document your claims, the more likely you are to get all you demand quickly and smoothly. Here are a few suggestions:

- **Establish an accident file**. Your Accident Notebook should have a copy of your insurance policy and all other records pertaining to the accident as they accumulate.

- **Maintain a chronological logbook**. In your logbook you can document any actions taken on your claim. For example, you would log the date and time of calls, whom you spoke with, briefly noting the substance of the conversation. You would also log all medical treatment, log the dates letters were mailed or received with a brief description of content, etc. (Not many are disciplined enough to maintain this but it will be a tremendous help if your claim blooms into a lawsuit.)

- **Keep copies of all documents**. Keep copies of all correspondence, bills, accident reports, claims forms, contracts, written reports from doctors, etc. that pertain to your claim. Maintaining your own files on the claim is very important.

In the legal and insurance worlds, paperwork is your friend. Establishing a comprehensive paper trail, documenting your accident experience from the moment the glass settles until you endorse your settlement check, is one of the best ways you can take control of your own recovery process. It is with these documents that you prove you deserve all that you ask for.

With this in mind, let's look at the three scenarios of the claims process.

SCENARIO 1: DEFENDING CLAIMS AGAINST YOUR POLICY

Your insurance company is your legal representative for claims against your liability policy. You pay your insurer to assume legal and economic responsibility for the damages you cause in an accident. Although the company does most of the work, you also have a role to play in helping the company defend against these claims.

Your insurance policy spells out all the contractual duties you owe your company when you are involved in an accident. You should be familiar with the specifics of your individual policy because violating some aspect of your duty to the insurance company can slow the claims process and even jeopardize your coverage. Your primary responsibilities are simply reporting accidents promptly and co-operating with your company's investigation. If you are irresponsible and uncooperative, the company might refuse to defend you and fail to renew your coverage when your policy expires. Usually the conditions are fairly straightforward and easy to comply with.

Most states have some form of "unfair claims practices act" that sets minimum standards for companies to follow when settling claims. Since these laws usually require companies to act within a specific time period, they need to be informed as soon as possible after the accident.

Initially, your insurance company will need to know how the accident happened; the name, address, and phone number of other people involved in the accident and of any witnesses; and they will need a copy of the police report. These items are described in detail in Chapter 2.

Your insurer will be best able to defend you if you keep its representatives informed. Treat your company's representatives as if they are your high paid attorneys. When you receive any legal notices or papers concerning a case against your policy, send your company copies. If another insurance company or an opposing party's attorney requests information from you having to do with a claim against your policy, clear it with your insurance company before providing any information. If possible, everything should go through your insurer, rather than from you directly.

You can help your insurer most by cooperating with the investigation and being available when needed. You might be asked to give a deposition which is a formal, recorded testimony about the accident, performed under oath. There might be other personal information, such as your medical history or driving record, which the insurance company might need. Unless you have a legitimate legal reason for withholding certain facts, your insurer should have access to any information related to the case, some of which might be very personal.

Dealing With Claims Problems in Scenario 1

Generally, there are only two types of problems which occur concerning liability coverage: either your insurance company refuses to defend you (denies coverage) or you are underinsured.

Insurer denies coverage. Insurers can refuse to provide liability coverage for many reasons, some of which are: (1) if you, the policyholder, intentionally caused the accident; (2) if the accident occurred while you were "engaged in business" and the policy does not cover this type of use (work related accidents and worker's compensation will be discussed later in this chapter); or (3) if you misrepresent "any material fact" relating to the insurance when the policy was originally obtained or at any time during the policy period.

Whether your liability coverage is withdrawn for legitimate reasons or not, the best advice we can give you is to consult with an attorney who specializes in insurance law. If you did something to truly jeopardize your coverage you need professional help to protect your personal assets. Insurance companies rarely refuse liability coverage without good reason, but if your insurer is acting in bad faith, a knowledgeable attorney is your most appropriate advocate.

A skilled attorney might be able to get a court judgment compelling your insurer to provide coverage and defend you. Otherwise, an attorney might at least be able to convince the company to represent you against the other driver's claims, leaving the question of who pays damages for later determination. In the extreme situation, you may have to hire an attorney to defend you against the other driver's claim and sue your insurer for coverage separately. In any case, denial of insurance coverage is a very serious issue which you shouldn't accept without professional advice and assistance.

You are underinsured. If you think you are underinsured — the claim against you is realistically worth a good deal more than the limits of your policy and therefore your personal assets might be in jeopardy — consider getting additional legal assistance in the case as early as possible. For example, if you caused $60,000 in property damage but only have $25,000 in property damage liability coverage, your insurer is only responsible for a maximum of $25,000; the remaining balance of $35,000 comes out of your pocket.

The insurance company is legally obliged to attempt to settle the claim within the limits of your policy, which would leave your pocketbook untouched, but there are times when it might be unable to do so. There also are times when the insurance company, in its zeal to minimize its losses, might refuse to settle the case within your policy limits.

This situation potentially puts you and your insurance company at odds. If the company does not negotiate in good faith, it may be liable for the full amount of the trial judgment, regardless of your policy limits. If this is the scenario, it is in your best interest to get professional legal assistance as early in the process as possible.

Your best protection, if you think you might be under-insured, is to discuss the case with your insurance company at the onset. The claims representative should have a good feel for whether the case might exhaust the limits of your policy. If inadequate insurance coverage is a possibility, stay involved in the settlement negotiations. Legally, insurance companies must act in good faith to settle claims regardless of the dollar value and your policy limits. If you are at all concerned with the way your insurer is handling your case you should consult an outside attorney.

SCENARIO 2: MAKING A CLAIM AGAINST YOUR OWN INSURANCE POLICY

Your own insurance policy, with MedPay or PIP, comprehensive/collision, and uninsured motorist coverages, is available to help pay for your damages resulting from the accident. When all goes well, you simply provide the company with proof of *reasonable* expenses and it is obliged to reimburse you up to the limits of your coverage.

The first step in making a claim on your policy is notifying your insurer of the accident. The company will want all the usual information pertaining to the accident as discussed in Scenario 1 above and in Chapter 2. The claims representative should also explain the claims process at this time. Each insurer has its own particular requirements for policyholder claims and the procedures may also vary with the type of claim.

For car repair costs, for example, some companies will issue a check immediately after an adjuster personally inspects the damages. Other companies use an appraiser who reports the damage estimate to a claims office. You would then receive a check from a central office. Still others pay based on cost estimates obtained from independent automotive repair shops. Medical services are usually handled differently in that most insurers need only be billed for necessary treatment.

Obviously, it is important that you understand your company's claims requirements as well as the limits of your individual coverage. Your primary responsibility in the claims process is making sure you understand what your insurer will pay for based on your policy limits and the proper procedures for making a claim. If you are not sure how your company wants you to get your car fixed, or whether your MedPay covers acupuncture or therapeutic massage without a physician's recommendation, ask before you act. You cannot ask too many questions of your claims representative and by keeping yourself informed you can avoid many of the common claims problems.

Dealing With Claims Problems in Scenario 2

Sometimes the claims process works smoothly; you get your accident expenses paid quickly and everyone is satisfied. Other times, it might feel like you are trying to "squeeze blood out of a turnip." Potential difficulties come in several forms, all of which can be frustrating and disconcerting.

Inadequate collision/comprehensive reimbursement. Your insurance company may haggle over the amount it is willing to pay to fix your car. It may seem silly that insurers quibble over a few hundred dollars, but they do because the dollars add up when you consider the millions of claims they process annually. The trouble comes when the company either offers too little to replace or fully restore your vehicle.

You are not helpless to your insurance company's judgment. First, and most important, the amount of money you accept is negotiable. Your insurer is trying to minimize its pay-out, so generally its offer will be on the low side of a fair price. If you feel that you are being offered too little, you should think of all you can legitimately do to prove that you are entitled to more.

For example, if your car had expensive alloy wheels, a special paint job, or anything unusual to make it worth more, make sure your company is aware of it. Preferably, you do this before an accident by notifying your company in writing and with pictures, but receipts or pictures after the fact will help.

When your car is totaled, you receive your company's estimate of its "market worth" which is most likely much less than it will cost to replace the car. It works as though you are selling your car to the insurance company; the price is negotiable. Again, if you have documentation of special equipment, you should receive more; if your car was in bad shape, you will get less. Since the value of the settlement is negotiable, take a look in a Kelly Blue Book, NADA Guide, Black Book, or check your local newspaper's classified ads to get an idea of the going price for your vehicle. Realistically, you will not recover replacement value, but you should be adequately compensated.

Medical costs exceed coverage limits. This is not as uncommon as you might think; $10,000 of MedPay may not cover the complete treatment of a serious whiplash. When your insurer has paid to the limit of your MedPay or PIP, the company has fulfilled its obligation to you, and you must look elsewhere to pay for your continued medical treatment. Some alternatives are other forms of health insurance, paying out of your own pocket, foregoing needed treatment, making a claim on your uninsured motorist coverage (if circumstances apply), and making a claim against the other driver's insurance policy. The first four choices are straightforward, although we certainly hope no one ignores their treatment needs.

The last alternative, making a claim against the other driver's liability coverage, can, unfortunately, take several months or even years (see Scenario 3, below). A Federal Government study (performed by The Department of Transportation) found that for losses over $2,500, the average settlement took nineteen months. If you follow this route and you do reach your coverage limit while waiting for the settlement dollars, you do not have to stop receiving medical care. Most medical professionals will agree to take a "lien" against your settlement in return for their services.

A lien is a legal claim on property for payment of a debt. In other words, your doctor, chiropractor, or other health-care professional will exchange services for a legal claim against your insurance settlement. When you settle your claim, you pay off the liens. Some medical offices will require a simple legal agreement. Others will work directly with the attorney working on your claim. Many medical professionals will accept this type of arrangement and have no problem waiting for payment.

Insurer terminates medical coverage before policy limits are met. An insurance company may decide, at some point during your recovery, that treatment is excessive and stop paying your medical bills. For example, the company may decide that reasonable treatment for whiplash should only cost $2,000; claims above that amount are scrutinized and often refused. So, when you exceed this arbitrary limit, your coverage may be in jeopardy.

To evaluate the "true" extent of claimed injuries, the insurer may ask the policyholder to submit to an examination by an insurance company-paid physician who may be acutely aware of the company's desire to limit coverage. Frequently in this situation, the diagnosis supports disallowing coverage. Insurers may also ask to examine the policyholder's previous medical history and refuse coverage based on physical conditions that existed before the accident.

As in the situation where coverage limits are exceeded, options available to the policyholder whose insurer terminates medical coverage are other forms of health insurance, paying out of your own pocket, foregoing needed treatment, making a claim on your uninsured motorist coverage (if circumstances apply), and making a claim against the other driver's insurance policy.

In addition, there are a few ways that you can persuade your insurer to provide full coverage as stated in your policy. First, try to find a more sympathetic ear in the company. If it is your claims representative who is refusing coverage, contact his/her supervisor. For this to be successful, you need complete and accurate documentation of injuries and legitimately prescribed care. A sad emotional story will simply not work. Make sure you document all communication with the insurance company. Don't expect a miraculous change of mind, but it doesn't hurt to try.

If you feel strongly that your claim is legitimate and your insurer is unfairly limiting coverage, you may want to notify the insurance commission in your state. Each state office has its own procedure for filing complaints. Most insurance companies pay attention to inquiries from their state watchdog, but if your complaint is without merit, even this type of pressure will not help.

Finally, if you have an attorney (and you may want to consider hiring one in this situation), include him/her in the process, especially if you are asked to take a physical examination. Sometimes an attorney can get the insurance company's attention more easily than a policyholder. If necessary, you and your attorney may even decide to sue your own company for unpaid claims.

SCENARIO 3: MAKING A CLAIM AGAINST ANOTHER DRIVER'S INSURANCE POLICY

Your insurance policy only offers limited potential for economic recovery. It pays for vehicle repairs and medical bills, but does not compensate you for lost wages and general damages (pain and suffering). While some no-fault systems provide limited lost wage recovery, in most circumstances, making a claim against the other driver's liability coverage is the only way to obtain more complete damage compensation.

If you were not at fault (and in no-fault states when the laws allow it), the other driver's insurance normally offers the largest economic support potential for your recovery. That's the good news. The bad news is that you either have to make the claim on your own or hire a personal injury attorney to do it for you. Your insurance company has very little to do with claims you make against the other driver's policy.

As mentioned above, your insurance company can only go after the opposing company (the process of subrogation) to recoup the amount it paid you, if any, under your collision/comprehension and MedPay/PIP coverages. If you want to recover lost wages, general damages, and any other legitimate loses, or if you want to forego a claim on your own policy and recover the full amount of damages, you must make a claim against the other driver's policy.

In deciding whether to jump into the claims process on your own, consider whether investing the time, effort, and emotional energy it takes to deal with the other insurer on your own is worth the 33% you keep by not having to pay attorney's fees. Exactly how much time and energy needed is difficult to predict. There are many factors at play, many of which you have little control over, but it is safe to assume it will not be easy. If you are bashful, get frustrated easily, or think you might have trouble persistently pursuing your claim, get professional assistance. If you do have an attorney, he/she will be your link to the process. Most insurance companies, even your own, will not give much information to you directly once you have legal representation. If you have an attorney handling your case, you get information on your case through him/her.

Many experts suggest that in situations where fault is at issue or more than two cars are involved, especially if there are no witnesses, you should seek legal assistance immediately. Too often, stories get twisted and accident victims get caught in the middle of two insurers trying to avoid liability for the damages.

If you do hire an attorney, let him/her handle all communication with the other insurance company. Some claims representatives can be very clever in their attempts to limit their company's liability. Before giving a statement, clear it with your attorney. Before accepting a settlement offer, clear it with your attorney. Before signing any paperwork, clear it with your attorney. When you do give your statement to the other company, have your attorney present. You are paying for legal advice — take advantage of it.

Nothing prevents you from testing the waters yourself and starting the claim on your own and hiring an attorney if needed at some point down the line. While pursuing the settlement on your own, you can still consult with an attorney at any time for an hourly fee without hiring him or her for the whole process. If it gets too difficult, or if it looks as though a lawsuit is necessary, you can then employ a professional.

In whatever manner you decide to proceed, **keep good records of everything related to the claim**, especially if you handle the case on your own. The better your documentation of medical treatment, lost wages, property damage, communication with insurers and attorneys, and everything else, the easier it is to prove your claims and the smoother the settlement process will proceed. Keeping track of who you are speaking with and for what reason is important because the process can be confusing.

Whether it is you or your attorney making the claim, the process is basically the same. Lawyers do not have a secret formula, but many have experience and emotional distance from the claim, which helps. The first step is making contact with the other driver's insurance company. This initial contact puts the company on notice that a claim has been made on one of its policies and thus an investigation is in order.

Usually, the company will assign a claims representative to the case, who will then gather all the information needed to establish fault and thus liability. If possible, it is this person with whom you want to develop a good working relationship because he/she will be the one you negotiate with.

Depending on the timing, your call may or may not be the first the company has heard of the accident. The company will need time to take statements from all involved and conduct an investigation, so do not expect much from the first contact other than setting the gears in motion. If you are persistent in asking questions, you ought to be able to get the information you need about the company's claims process. Be sure to ask what type of documentation the company requires and what you can do to expedite the process. Be cordial, patient, and do not be afraid to keep asking questions until you understand. The initial contact will give you a flavor of the company, whether the claims representative is friendly or brusque, helpful or aloof, knowledgeable and organized, or incompetent.

If there is any question of who is at fault, (for instance, if your story differs from the other driver's on whether the light was green, red, or yellow) it is initially the job of the insurance companies to investigate and decide the issue. To establish fault, claims representatives use police reports (if obtained), statements of those involved in the accident, witness statements (if available), and may even visit the scene or employ accident reconstruction experts.

Most claims representatives have little formal training; rather, they rely on common sense and on-the-job experience in their work. What this means to you is that your presentation of your version of the case is very important, especially your accuracy and credibility. The best advice is: think before you speak, be honest, and make sure you are being understood (if the circumstances are complicated, pictures or drawings can be very helpful). Do not be vindictive and self-righteous, it leaves a bad impression. Remember, the point is to resolve the issue of fault, so that your economic recovery proceeds as quickly as possible.

If the fault determination is controversial, both insurance companies will undoubtedly be involved since both you and the other driver are probably making competing claims on each other's policies. Again, if the situation gets too complicated, consider getting legal assistance. When fault cannot be agreed upon, the case may eventually bloom into a lawsuit. While the investigation proceeds, your insurance company might not keep you updated so you may have to pursue the information yourself.

Once fault is determined, or if there is no dispute about who is to blame (the other driver has admitted fault and his insurer agrees on accepting liability), the dollar value of the settlement still needs to be worked out. Normally, the other driver's insurer will not pay you piecemeal; rather, payment comes when you agree on a complete settlement. Some companies will pay for property damages quickly, then later, when a final settlement is determined, pay the balance of special and general damages.

To reach a settlement, you need to know the value of your claim. Obviously, you will want reimbursement for all your bills, lost wages, and possibly some general damage compensation. Lawyers and insurance companies use the phrase "permanent and stationary" to describe the state of your recovery when you are ready to put a realistic value to your claim. In most cases, this means your medical treatment must be complete, or at least the full extent of your injuries and the necessary treatment must be identified.

Healing from an accident can take time and the type and amount of treatment necessary is not always apparent when an injury is initially diagnosed. For example, serious ligament damage may take several months and multiple treatment methods to treat and stabilize to the point that a good estimate of cost can be obtained. Post-traumatic stress disorder cannot be officially diagnosed until symptoms persist for over a month and then several months of treatment may be essential. Generally, you should not settle your claim until you have a reliable measure of the full extent of your damages because an insurance company will not pad a settlement to protect you from some unknown complication. Patience is essential to avoid cheating yourself out of needed economic support.

This does not mean that an aggressive claims representative will not try to settle quickly and for as little as possible, especially if it might save the company money. In fact, some might be fairly aggressive in trying to get you to settle. One way to give yourself time and avoid verbal misunderstandings is to ask politely for all communication to be in writing.

Throughout the process, it is important that you seriously weigh the cost/benefit of each settlement offer.

Sometimes a dollar in hand is worth more than the potential of two down the road, especially if later means you have to share some percentage with an attorney. Remember, you also have the option of utilizing liens (discussed above in Scenario 2) against your settlement as a form of payment for most services, so you should not have to forego medical treatment.

Meanwhile, the economic burden of recovering from the accident falls on your shoulders, with some help from your own insurance, depending on your coverage and if you decide to use it. Even with your own insurance, the economic pressure can be heavy. It is not unusual to lose several days or even months of wages and exhaust the limits of your MedPay/PIP coverage while negotiating a settlement with the other driver's insurance company. Some insurance companies have been known to abuse this situation by prolonging the negotiation process, hoping that you will give in to the economic pressure and accept a less than equitable settlement.

Dick

One evening, I was broad-sided by a drunk driver as he was driving home from a Super Bowl party. His car was totaled but because I was wearing my seat belt, I escaped with some torn ligaments in my lower back and a few cuts and bruises. Normally, I make a living delivering furniture, but I was unable to work for several months while my back was healing.

Within a few days following the crash, the other driver's insurer contacted me. He assured me that since the crash was clearly the drunk driver's fault I would be taken care of with little fuss.

Early the next morning, I was surprised to find the claims representative at my door. He was very sympathetic and after talking with me about the wreck, *he presented me with a check for $20,000 (my car alone was worth about $12,000). He said the check was mine if I signed "a simple claims release form." In fact, the form was quite simple, only two pages long, explaining that by accepting the check and signing the form, I was giving up all future rights to claims related to the crash.*

I had never held a check for $20,000 and I certainly was tempted to accept it. I had health insurance and automobile insurance to cover some of the expenses, but I really didn't know how long I would be out of work or how much my medical bills would be. The claims representative's eagerness bothered me enough to refuse the offer. The claims representative told me to think it over. He even left the check and the release form on the kitchen table on his way out.

I was prudent enough to ask around. I called my doctor and my own insurance company to get advice. They both told me to make copies of the check and the release form and send the papers back to the insurance company with a letter explaining that I felt it was in my best interest to wait until my condition stabilized before I accepted any settlement.

Over the next few months I had several abrupt and unsatisfying conversations with the claims representative when I tried to ask questions or give a progress report. Nine months after the crash, when my condition was predictable, I sent a settlement package to the claims representative asking for $45,000 to resolve the claim. It turned out that my medical bills, lost wages, and property damages totaled over $38,000.

The claims representative repeatedly told me that the company had made its final offer at $20,000 and that there was nothing more to discuss. In the meantime, I still needed periodic medical treatment, but my MedPay limit was exhausted and my health insurance was only paying 80%. By this time, I had missed several weeks wages and was at the end of my savings, and all in all, I wanted the wreck out of my life.

Over the next two months, we dickered back and forth with little progress. The claims representative was willing to pay $25,000 tops but that didn't even cover my losses.

Luckily, I contacted an attorney before the statute of limitations prevented a lawsuit (one year where I lived), and we filed a lawsuit. Even with an attorney and a lawsuit, it wasn't until 18 months following the crash that the lawyer was able to negotiate an agreeable settlement.

When you have a good idea of the value of your claim and are ready to actively negotiate, you need to gather all your documentation into a "settlement memorandum." This document is a several page letter you send to the claims representative describing the accident, your injuries (physical, emotional, and economic) and treatment, and most importantly, concluding with a monetary demand for settlement. A sample settlement memorandum is presented in Appendix A, but make sure it includes the following:

- **Written reports from medical professionals.** Ask each medical professional from whom you have received ongoing therapy to prepare a report which includes your medical history related to the accident, diagnosis, course of treatment, prognosis, and cost.

You may have to pay a small fee for this but it is a persuasive addition to copies of the bills you enclose with the memo.

- **Employer lost-wage letter.** Have your employer write a letter documenting your missed work days and lost wages because of your injuries. Even if you were granted paid sick leave or took vacation pay to recover, you are still entitled to compensation if the accident was the cause.

- **Property damage documentation**. Document your property damage with pictures, bills, or whatever is necessary to justify your costs, if you have not already settled this aspect of your claim.

- **Logbook excerpts.** You have your accident diary and/or logbook to help you review the recovery period and determine a reasonable general damage assessment. You can quote or copy passages to include in the memo if you think it will help your claim. You are not trying to win any theatrical awards but if you truly suffered, the law allows you fair compensation.

It may take some time for the claims representative to review your memo and he/she may ask for more documentation and/or to review your medical records. You may need to authorize access to your records. If you do, note **clearly**, that the authorization is limited to only those medical records relating to the accident or covering a specific time period. Claims representatives can be very imaginative in finding prior history to suggest that an injury existed before the accident, thus avoiding liability.

Do not hesitate to consult with an attorney if you are concerned about your privacy or if some requests seem unreasonable. In fact, this may be an area where you want professional guidance. If you do not want an attorney to take over your claim in its entirety, an alternative is hiring him/her as a "self-help law coach." With this arrangement you would pay by the hour for consultation only in the specific areas where you need it. (See Chapter 9 for more details on consulting with or hiring an attorney.)

Settlement negotiations are the most unpredictable aspect of your claim. Even if you are honest and straightforward in your demands, you may meet some strong resistance in settling. Know that there is no such thing as a "final offer" until you have received a check and signed a release. If you are a salesperson or a barterer at heart you might enjoy this aspect of the process. If not, hang on to your principles and be prepared to hire an attorney (they love to haggle, that is why they do what they do).

In the end, deciding to accept an offer will depend on what is fair and reasonable based on your injuries and your immediate needs balanced against the value of cases similar to yours in your area of the country. Once you reach some agreement on a fair economic settlement, the insurance company pays you and you sign a "release of liability" form, giving up all legal rights to future claims against the insurer and the other driver that pertain to the accident.

If you cannot find a mutually acceptable settlement amount, you will have to sue the insurance company. You may have to file a lawsuit anyway to avoid statute of limitation problems even though negotiations are proceeding as they should and/or your injuries have not yet stabilized. If a lawsuit is inevitable, numerous self-help legal resources are available if you want to continue handling your case without professional assistance. Joseph L. Matthews has written an excellent resource book for those who choose to handle their own claim called *How To Win Your Personal Injury Claims*. It is available from Nolo Press.

The paperwork associated with filing a lawsuit is cumbersome and technical although not impossible for the layperson, but (and it is a big "but") if you have not been able to settle with the other company thus far, you probably need expert tactical assistance. If it comes to this, we suggest that you seriously consider hiring an attorney.

Preparing for a lawsuit does not stop the negotiations, but it can add an acrid flavor to the recovery process for all involved. You will get a firsthand view of the "adversarial" legal system which few find is a pleasant experience. For the other driver's insurance company, defending against your lawsuit is expensive. However, rather than working in your favor by helping to force a settlement, the increased cost pressure frequently backfires. The other driver's insurer can become singularly focused on ruthlessly proving that you deserve little to nothing in compensation. To do this, the insurer's attorneys thoroughly investigate the validity of your damage claims, as well as any pertinent personal history. This phase of the pre-trial preparation is called the "discovery" process. Much of your life becomes an open book to the opposing party and to a full courtroom if your case goes to trial. If you value your privacy this can be an uncomfortable experience.

Your attorney should be aware of all communication between you and the opposing party. In fact, all requests should go through your legal representative. Insurance investigators can be quite creative in the way they try to get information, so avoid discussing the accident or your injuries with strangers without first clearing it with your attorney.

At some point, you will have to give a formal statement, called a deposition, to the opposing party's attorneys. Your attorney should brief you on what to expect beforehand, but you will likely feel that you are being interrogated by the enemy. Your attorney should also be present if you are examined by an insurance company doctor. Keep your attorney informed of everything and do not volunteer information to the other side, once you are working within the context of a lawsuit. The opposing party will capitalize on the smallest detail to minimize or disprove your claims.

Meanwhile, negotiations will continue based on the information unearthed through depositions, physical exams, and other inquiries during the discovery phase. Most cases (over 95%) settle before a formal courtroom trial because, contrary to Perry Mason episodes, very little new information is disclosed during trial. By the time the case is ready for trial all the facts needed to form an equitable settlement are present. What is lacking is an agreement.

If the parties cannot settle on their own, they meet with the judge assigned to the case in a pre-trial conference. In this meeting, the judge reviews the case with the attorneys without the formalities of the courtroom setting. An experienced judge can make suggestions that help the attorneys find common ground for a settlement. Nevertheless, there will always be cases that must be argued in the courtroom.

The trial itself will normally only last a few days. But in complicated situations the proceedings can go on for quite some time. Even during the trial it is not uncommon for the parties to reach a settlement, ending the case. Only a small fraction of insurance claims are actually tried to completion before a judge or jury. And only a handful of court judgments in these cases are appealed to the next level of the judicial system.

Dealing With Claims Problems in Scenario 3

What is your case worth? If your expectations are high, you will have difficulty settling your case and will likely be dissatisfied with a court judgment. Alternatively, if you accept too little, you may not be able to afford the treatment and time away from work necessary to recover fully.

In many situations, you will be able to settle relatively quickly if you value your case realistically.

Unfortunately, estimating the value of your case is not an exact science. The easy part is totaling up all your "special damages" (the better your documentation, the more you get). This doesn't mean the insurance company will agree that your claim warrants this amount, but at least it is based on tangible numbers like medical bills, lost wages, etc.

Putting a reliable figure to general damages is, at best, a very "iffy" task. The type of injury, the personal appeal of the accident victim (widows and children get more sympathy), the area of the country, the quirks of the claims representative, internal policies of the insurer, the insurance coverage limits, the personal assets of the party at fault, etc. all affect the potential recovery. Some experts suggest that 1 to 5 times the total medical billing is a fair estimate of general damages, but these figures are arbitrary. Most of all, you need to evaluate your own needs, based on legitimate accident injuries, and consider how long and how hard you are willing to fight.

If you are handling the claim on your own, you might want to hire an attorney as a "self-help law coach" to get a professional estimate on your claim's value. It can't hurt to show your settlement memorandum to a personal injury attorney to get suggestions and a sanity check on your demands. You can arrange to pay the attorney by the hour as it shouldn't take much time. Before doing this, make sure the attorney is in favor of your handling the case on your own and knows you are paying for a consultation and not hiring him/her. Whatever the estimate, also consider that if you settle on your own, you do not have to pay attorney's fees (usually 33% of the settlement value – possibly more if the case goes to court). So if you accept less than the attorney estimates, you might still come out ahead.

Overriding the whole evaluation is the ability of the other driver and/or his insurance company to pay. If the other driver only has minimal insurance coverage and no personal assets, it doesn't matter how much you think you deserve; at best you will get the full insurance coverage limits.

Moreover, you have to temper your expectations with the settlement offer you get from the claims representative. Based on the initial investigations and in comparison to all the other cases the claims representative has handled, he/she will estimate the value of your claim. Whether it is fair to you and your individual circumstance or not, it is from this point that you must negotiate. If the offer is extremely different from yours, it is your job to convince the claims representative you deserve more, which may not be a simple or easy task. A claims representative with hundreds of cases worth of experience may be very fixed in his/her valuation.

Plus, each claims representative has a limited settlement authority. A settlement amount above a certain value (it could be anything from $1,000 to $50,000 or more) must have supervisory approval. Each person up the hierarchy has his/her own limited authority, so the more you demand, the more complicated the approval process becomes.

Time limits on filing a lawsuit. You must file a lawsuit within a specific amount of time following the accident or else the "statute of limitations" expires and you lose the right to sue altogether. The statute of limitations varies in each state. In most states, adults have a full year following the accident in which to initiate a lawsuit, but for minors, the right to sue often remains open until they are 18 years old. There are other time limits governing the paperwork associated with a lawsuit as well.

Claims against government agencies. Accidents involving private citizens and government owned vehicles (fire trucks, police cars, snow clearing vehicles, etc.) are not unusual. Each government entity has its own rules and paperwork associated with liability claims. Some municipalities require notice of a claim within as little as 30 days or you lose the legal right to recover. Your best bet is to find a competent, knowledgeable attorney immediately following the accident because the laws which shape and limit government liability are abundant and complex.

On the job automobile accidents and workers' compensation. If your accident occurred while on the job, get an attorney to handle your case and do your best to get healthy. Actually, you need two attorneys, one to handle your workers' compensation claim and one to handle your claim against the other driver's insurer. We suggest this because your case has the potential of being very complex, frustrating, and lengthy.

Workers' compensation laws confuse the claims process immensely. Workers' compensation is supposed to provide medical and wage loss benefits to employees who are injured in a work-related incident. The rules are like no-fault insurance in the sense that if you are injured on the job, you are eligible for limited compensation, regardless of who or what caused the accident.

The workers' compensation system is less than perfect. The biggest complaint is that benefits available to injured workers are miserably inadequate, especially if injuries are severe. Often, an injured worker must hire an experienced attorney to wade through the appeals process to get a sufficient settlement.

The intricacies don't stop there, however. An option, if you were not at fault in your accident, is to make a claim against the other driver's liability policy. Go ahead and shake your head in disbelief, but you might need a separate attorney for this claim. The reason is because some insurers are willing to fight against settling a claim when workers' compensation is available. Many attorneys specialize; an experienced workers' compensation attorney is not necessarily a proficient personal injury attorney and vice versa. When more than one source of compensation is available, i.e., workers' compensation and other private insurance, each insurer points its finger at all the other funds available to heal your economic wounds and fights to the end to limit its own liability.

Finally, your two attorneys may disagree on who should be arguing for what and for how much. Each case has its own peculiarities; there are no set rules on what workers' compensation should pay and what other insurance is responsible for. Let your attorneys haggle it out; better them than you, as long as you eventually get your expenses paid.

CONCLUSION

This chapter contains an intimidatingly large amount of information, which is understandable because the insurance claims process can be quite complicated. Nevertheless, it is information which empowers you to make healthy choices in your recovery process. It is important that you do your best to understand how the system functions. Here are some of the important facts to remember concerning your economic recovery:

- There are very few accident situations where you are better off leaving your insurance company out of the picture.

- The better you document your claim, the more likely you will be satisfied with your insurance settlement.

- Three separate scenarios compose the claims process: making a claim on your own insurance coverage, helping your insurer defend you against claims on your liability coverage, and making a claim against another driver's insurance policy.

- Economic recovery is often a very slow process, especially if you make a claim against another driver's insurance policy.

- The more comprehensively you document your injuries and your recovery process, the more likely you will find success with your claims.

- Consider each settlement offer carefully; one dollar in your pocket now may or may not be worth more than two down the road.

- You do not necessarily need an attorney for your recovery, but there are some situations where it is helpful.

NOTES

CHAPTER 9

LEGAL ASSISTANCE

A LAWYER CAN BE YOUR ALLY

Unfortunately, our adversarial "who is to blame" insurance claims system makes for some very difficult legal situations. In addition, the rudimentary forms of "no-fault" automobile insurance existing in a dozen or so states in the U.S. allow fault determining lawsuits in many situations. Therefore, hiring an attorney to assist you is sometimes a necessary option. This final chapter on economic recovery is meant to take some of the twists and blind curves out of the legal aspects of the insurance claims process.

WHEN TO SEEK LEGAL ASSISTANCE

You hire an attorney for his/her dexterity in working within the legal constraints of the system to promote your economic recovery. Without professional legal guidance, being in conflict with an insurance company can put you at an enormous disadvantage. After all, it is the full-time business of insurance companies to minimize the amount of money paid on their policies while this is probably the only time in your life you will be involved in this type of economic controversy.

Whether it is to your economic advantage to have professional legal representation depends on the circumstances. Most studies show that accident victims seek legal assistance more frequently as the amount of economic loss increases and that they obtain higher gross settlements than those without attorneys. But once attorneys fees and legal expenses are deducted, who ends up with more money, those with or those without professional assistance, depends on the specific facts of the claim.

For example, one study found that accident victims with back sprains received larger settlements when represented by an attorney while those who suffered a fracture of a weight-bearing bone did better economically if they did not have legal representation. The point is that there isn't a clear advantage one way or another. You have to weigh other factors when deciding whether to hire an attorney.

Another important point to consider is that attorney involvement usually prolongs the insurance settlement process. Although in some cases an attorney may be able to negotiate a larger net settlement, you will likely have to wait longer to receive the cash. One Rand Corporation study found that 75% of those victims who retained attorneys waited at least six months before reaching a settlement, but over 80% of those who handled their claim without legal representation settled within 180 days.

In another study conducted by the major insurance companies and published in 1979 by the All-Industry Research Advisory Committee, entitled, *Automobile Injuries and their Compensation in the United States*, they found that: "Bodily injury liability and uninsured motorist claimants who had economic losses of less than $500 received a larger amount from the auto insurance system if they were represented by an attorney, even after paying the estimated attorney fees. Claimants with economic losses greater than $2,000 received a larger net return if they were NOT represented by an attorney."

On the time involved to settle a case the insurance industry found that: "Attorney-represented claims took considerably longer to settle than nonrepresented claims. For bodily injury claims, those with attorneys took an average of 500 days from first report of injury to final payment, compared with an average of 100 days for nonrepresented claims. Similar differences were reported for uninsured motorists and personal injury protection claims as well." So think twice before you hire a lawyer; do an economic impact analysis of the alternatives to get some idea of how you might benefit in the end.

Finally, there is an unquantifable aspect to the process: do you feel confident enough in your own knowledge and ability to negotiate without professional assistance. As you can see from the previous two chapters, lawyers, at least skilled ones, need to have a good grasp of the technical workings of insurance policies and the nuances of the law where your accident took place. When you sign over 30 to 50% of your insurance settlement to an attorney, you are paying for more than his/her fancy clothes. Whether it is worth the time and headaches you avoid is a personal question only you can answer.

FINDING AN ATTORNEY

Always keep in mind that you pay an attorney to perform a service, and **it is your** money, property, and legal rights at stake. Finding an honest, competent, hard-working attorney may take some time, but it is well worth your effort to be discriminating. Friends, relatives, other accident victims, and medical professionals who deal with accident victims are the best sources for gathering names of respected attorneys. Be wary of hiring an attorney from a television advertisement. Some consumer rights legal groups also frown on prepaid legal plans. Finally, the number of attorneys listed in most phone books is overwhelming, but it is an ample source if you are willing to do some telephone interviewing.

As a rule, lawyers concentrate their practice in very specific areas of law. You want an attorney who specializes in personal injury cases. Your family friend who practices corporate law is not the best person to handle your automobile accident claim but might be a good source to help you find a personal injury specialist.

You must respect and feel comfortable with whomever you hire, so we strongly recommend that you interview a few attorneys before employing anyone. Avoid the temptation of selecting the first name you get. A few minutes on the phone asking some direct questions can save hours of future aggravation and disappointment.

Prepare yourself by writing down a few questions before you make initial telephone contact. Important things to consider during your first conversation are:

- Talk to the attorney you are considering directly, not a receptionist or a partner at the law firm.
- How many cases similar to yours has the attorney handled and with what success?
- What are the fees and are they negotiable? See discussion of fee arrangements below.
- Get names of prior clients, both pleased and dissatisfied.
- What percentage of the attorney's cases settle before trial and does he/she have trial experience? Arguing a case at trial is a learned art form. Experience is essential.
- What is the attorney's case load and how willing is he/she to answer questions throughout the process?

Some attorneys do not like interacting with clients, which is fine if that is what you want.

- Get the attorney to explain the claims process to you so you can hear him/her speak: Is he/she organized, do you understand the explanation, does he/she seem to be knowledgeable?

- Does the attorney carry malpractice insurance?

- You will also have to explain your circumstances and why you are looking for legal assistance. Does the attorney ask you intelligent questions as you are explaining?

- Ask him or her to explain what kinds of problems might arise during the settlement process.

- If you like the answers you have received, schedule an in-person interview.

You will know whether you can work with this attorney fairly quickly. Do not hire someone you feel uneasy with regardless of how much money he/she got for a friend or how enthusiastic he/she seems. HALT, a national organization dedicated to legal reform, suggests that before you actually meet with an attorney, contact your state disciplinary agency (often the "attorney grievance" section within the state bar association) to find out if the attorney has ever been publicly disciplined and to ensure that the lawyer is licensed to practice law in your state.

You should go into the initial attorney-client interview with three goals in mind: you want to ensure that the attorney can confidently handle your case, to understand clearly the services you are paying for, and to know how much you will be charged. Don't be afraid to ask whatever questions you think appropriate.

At the same time, the attorney should ask you to describe the details of the accident and your injuries. You want your case evaluated realistically and you want some assurance that the potential settlement makes the case worth an attorney's time. You should leave this interview with the attorney's estimate of the value of your case and knowing whether you want to hire him or her.

LEGAL FEES

There are three types of fee arrangements that lawyers use: hourly fees, flat fees, and contingency fees. If you are hiring a lawyer to defend you against a lawsuit you will normally pay by the hour. If you are handling your claim yourself, you can still use an attorney as a "self-help law coach," paying by the hour for advice in specific areas or to look over your paperwork. You will most likely pay on an hourly basis for this type of service.

A flat fee arrangement is usually used for routine legal issues such as uncontested divorces, preparation of a simple will, or incorporation of a business, and is normally not an option in the accident context.

The vast majority of personal injury claims against an insurance company are handled on a contingency fee basis. The contingency fee gives the lawyer a percentage of the settlement. The attorney risks the fee on his/her ability to recover damages for you. The larger the settlement, the more the attorney gets paid. Likewise, the attorney does not get paid if he/she cannot negotiate a settlement or win damages at trial.

At first glance it seems that attorneys take a big gamble with contingency fees. In reality, they rarely accept cases in which much risk is involved. If there is a genuine question of fault, or if there is a moderate chance that you will not be legally entitled to a recovery, your case will have to be worth a good deal of money before most personal injury attorneys will accept it on a contingency fee basis.

Although the fees may range from 15% to 50%, the customary contingency fee is 33% of the settlement. Some attorneys use a sliding scale where the percentage increases as the case moves from pre-trial settlement (perhaps 25%), to trial (increasing to 35%), and then on appeal (as high as 45%). Others might use a sliding scale based on the size of the settlement; for example, 33% of the first $10,000, 25% for the next $25,000, and so on. Within the customary range, the fee schedule is negotiable.

In addition, most attorneys deduct expenses from the settlement. It is important to specify whether the expenses are deducted from the total settlement or from your portion alone. If expenses are deducted before the attorney takes his fee, you will keep more of your settlement. For example:

Expenses From Your Portion		Expenses From Total	
Total Award	$60,000	Total Award	$60,000
Lawyer Fee (33%)	$20,000	Expenses	$6,000
Remainder	$40,000	Remainder	$54,000
Expenses	-$6,000	Lawyer Fee(33%)	-$17,820
What you get	$34,000	What you get	$36,180

Recall that many insurance policies, through the process of subrogation, require that you reimburse your company for amounts it paid you under MedPay and/or collision coverage if you later receive a settlement covering these expenses from another insurer. You would want to be sure the attorney subtracts these subrogated amounts from your settlement before figuring the contingency fee, as well.

As you can see, attorney's fees and expenses can take a large bite out of your settlement. Accepting a smaller settlement without legal assistance may net you more money than paying the contingency fees of a personal injury attorney.

If you have handled a good portion of your claim on your own but now feel it is necessary to hire professional assistance, you may want to consider finding an attorney who will accept a limited or modified contingency fee like Sarah did:

Sarah

I was rear ended while stopped at an intersection and ended up with a pretty severe whiplash. My medical bills totaled almost $5,000 and I lost almost two months of wages because I couldn't sit in a chair for any length of time. I work as a legal secretary (unfortunately not for a personal injury specialist) and I am familiar with legal jargon and paperwork, so I decided to handle my insurance claim on my own.

Once I was sure of my damages, I sent a very thorough settlement package, with full documentation of my expenses and my compensation requirement to the other driver's insurer. I had high hopes that we would find a mutually agreeable number, but after a month of phone calls back and forth my patience deteriorated and I didn't want to subject myself to the claims adjuster's condescending manner. We were still about $10,000 apart and neither would budge.

I decided I'd had enough and found an attorney who agreed to take my case on a modified contingency basis. Since I had taken care of most of the paperwork (he complimented me on how complete the documentation was), he agreed that his contingency fee (35%) would be derived only from the amount in excess of what I had last been offered.

My initial demand was for $35,000, but by the time I went to the attorney the insurance company would only go as high as $25,000. It took some time, but eventually the attorney got my full request of $35,000. If I had used the traditional contingency fee arrangement the attorney would have taken his 35% from the whole $35,000 ($12,250), which would have left me with only $22,750. It wouldn't have been worth using an attorney under these circumstances.

Since we used the modified contingency fee, the attorney only took 35% of $10,000 (35% of the amount above the $25,000 offer). He got $3,500 and I kept $31,500.

Even if the attorney is unable to get you any money, you must still pay the expenses and costs related to the lawsuit. These include court filing fees, deposition charges, fees for expert witnesses, travel expenses, etc. The details should be specified in the agreement you make with the attorney. One thing to consider is putting a cap on these expenses and requiring the attorney to obtain your authorization before this limit is exceeded.

In all likelihood, an attorney will present you with a written contract specifying the terms of your agreement. **Review it carefully.** Pay attention to the details concerning fees, expenses, and particularly anything relating to the manner in which disputes will be resolved and the conditions and fees required to terminate the agreement before settlement.

PROBLEMS WITH AN ATTORNEY

The way to avoid problems with your lawyer is by selecting him/her carefully and by staying involved in the case. If problems do develop, no matter how trivial they may seem, address them as soon as they arise. If you wait or ignore them, chances are they will mushroom.

The most common problem is client and/or case neglect. Other difficult situations include: failure to obtain the statement of a key witness, neglecting to prepare you for a deposition or trial, agreeing to a settlement without your approval, withholding information to manipulate your decision on a settlement, suggesting you exaggerate or falsify injuries, missing filing deadlines, deducting exorbitant expense fees from the settlement, and the list goes on.

Lucy

Lucy's accident was clearly the fault of the other driver and he was adequately insured. Her injuries were moderate but not permanently disabling, including a fractured arm, concussion, whiplash, and mild psychological trauma. Lucy retained an attorney immediately after the accident because she was in no condition, either physically or emotionally, to handle the claim on her own. The attorney she hired worked at a large law firm which advertised personal injury claims as one of their specialties.

Lucy's injuries were slow to heal, she knew it would take some time before a settlement could be negotiated. She did not keep in touch with her attorney or monitor his progress in any way. When the settlement was finally reached for about $40,000, Lucy was shocked to receive a check for only $15,000. She figured that after the attorney deducted his 33% and perhaps two or three thousand in expenses, she would receive at least $25,000. It turned out that the attorney deducted over $10,000 in expenses.

Needless to say, Lucy was outraged, especially considering her medical bills totaled almost $10,000. After writing a number of letters to the senior part-

ners at the law firm and to the state bar, an investigation revealed that the attorney had grossly overcharged Lucy. They found that most of the expenses were fictitious. She eventually was paid the full $40,000 settlement by the very apologetic law firm.

The first step in resolving most problems is to try to talk it through with the attorney. Even if you misunderstood the circumstances and there really isn't a problem at all, you should at least be able to clarify the situation. Try to be straightforward, saying "I expected this or that," or "Is there any reason why this hasn't occurred?" This tone will be much more effective than argumentatively demanding "You were late with this, why hasn't it happened?" or worse yet, "I'll fire you or sue you if you don't shape up."

After you resolve the conflict, try to come to an agreement that will avoid the problem in the future. For example, if you are having trouble getting progress reports, set a specific time every week or two for you to call and discuss your case.

Put things in writing, whether it is a complaint or the details of a resolved problem. Obviously you want your business relationship to succeed, but it never hurts to have good documentation of problems if you later need to dismiss or sue the attorney.

If, for any reason, you decide to fire the attorney, you will normally have to pay for services and expenses to date, even under a contingency fee. Your contract may detail these arrangements, otherwise the attorney is entitled to reasonable compensation based on the services provided. If, on the other hand, the firing is for "good cause," you may not have to pay fees and perhaps have grounds for a malpractice suit. You may also want to provide information to the state bar so that they can initiate disciplinary action.

It might be worth your while to find a replacement attorney to continue working on your case (another good reason to keep your own files and copies of all insurance claim documents), so your case isn't compromised while you are taking care of your dissatisfaction with the original attorney. Also, finding an attorney who is willing to sue another attorney for malpractice is not as difficult as it used to be. Some lawyers even specialize in professional negligence cases. Hopefully, you will not have to address these kinds of issues.

CONCLUSION

You don't necessarily need an attorney to negotiate an equitable accident settlement; many people are perfectly able to handle their claims without a lawyer. Yet some people and some circumstances warrant professional assistance. The important points to consider when working with an attorney are:

- You should not decide to hire an attorney based on the promise of big money.

- Consider your ability and temperament; if you don't enjoy conflict or having to be aggressive, you should hire an attorney to pursue your claim.

- Select an attorney carefully and make sure you understand what you are paying for when you hire one.

- Keep informed of the progress on your claim and don't hesitate to clear up any concerns you have before your case is jeopardized.

Chapter 10

CONCLUSION

In her book *Codependent No More*, Melody Beatie tells a fable about a woman who went to live in a special religious temple, to study with a great spiritual leader. The woman wanted to learn all she could about life and the universe. The great spiritual leader gave her stacks of books and left her alone to study.

Once a day, the great spiritual leader would visit the woman in her little room. Each visit he would ask her the same question. He would ask, "Have you learned all there is to know yet?" Of course, each time he asked, she would answer with an honest and humble, "No, no I haven't." And each time, after she answered, he would whack her over the head with his bamboo cane.

This odd scene repeated itself for days and days, ending with the same painful slap with the bamboo cane. One day he asked his question and she answered with the same, "no, no I haven't." But this time, as he swung his cane she reached up and grabbed it out of his hand.

Thinking she would be kicked out of the temple for questioning the spiritual leader, she was surprised to see him smile for the first time.

"Congratulations," he said, "you now know everything you need to know."

"What do you mean?" she asked.

"I mean, you've realized that even though you don't know all there is to know, you can still stop the pain," he responded.

Sometimes this is what life feels like, at least the hard times. You know you have a problem, you know you want the problem to go away, but sometimes it can take time to figure out how to make it happen. While you are fumbling to come up with a successful strategy, you have to endure the bops on the head with a stick. In the meantime, you manage to coexist with the frustration, confusion, and discomfort.

Then one day you realize what needs to be done - reach out and grab the stick. Once past, it may be hard to remember what was so difficult to begin with.

We aren't trying to tell you that healing from an auto accident is easy, or that healing occurs overnight. Unfortunately, that is not the way it works. But what we do know is, with knowledge, courage, and a good bit of faith, you can make the healing happen much more quickly.

In the previous pages, we've given you the knowledge you need to stop the stick. At least if the stick has something to do with the physical, emotional, or economic trauma of an auto accident.

Now you know you have to pay attention to the way your body feels inside, not just how it looks in the mirror. You shouldn't have to live with chronic pain from an accident injury. Getting proper medical care means being an active participant in the healing process. Proper healing often entails an extensive, multi-faceted treatment plan.

You also now know that your accident experience can cause lasting psychological wounds. If not the accident itself, the lengthy recovery period can cause tremendous emotional strain. Now you know how to adjust to the extra weight the accident throws on your shoulders.

Finally, you now have a map to help chart your way through the twists and blind curves you must navigate to complete your economic recovery. Whether you do it on your own or with an attorney, you know what to expect from the system and how to make it work to your advantage.

No doubt having the recovery steps spelled out makes it a much less daunting process. Nevertheless, what we can't give you is the courage to take responsibility for your healing, and the faith to make it happen. These things must spring from that special place inside you.

Take a deep breath, reach out and grab the stick, and trust that you will find your way to health.

NOTES

RESOURCES

LEGAL

Washington Legal Foundation
1705 N St.
Washington, DC

California Coalition Against DUI (CADUI)
Sacramento, CA
(916) 444-8014

INSURANCE

Contact your State Government for its State Insurance Department's telephone number.

National Consumers League
815 15th Street, NW
Washington, DC 20005
202-639-8140

Insurance Information Institute
110 William Street
New York, NY 10038
800-221-4954
800-669-9200

National Insurance Consumer Helpline
800-942-4242

Insurance Crime Prevention Institute
15 Franklin Street
Westport, CT 06880
800-221-5715

DRINKING AND DRIVING

Citizens for Safe Drivers Against Drunk Drivers and Other Chronic Offenders
P.O. Box 42018
Washington, DC 20015
301-469-6282

Mothers Against Drunk Driving (MADD)
511 E. John Carpenter Frwy, Suite 700
Irving, TX 75062
214-744-6233
800-GET-MADD

Remove Intoxicated Drivers
P.O. Box 520
Schenectady, NY 12301
518-372-0034

Students Against Driving Drunk
P.O. Box 800
Marlborough, MA 01752
508-481-3568

Insurance Institute for Highway Safety
10005 N. Glebe Rd.
Arlington, VA 22201
703-247-1500

National Clearinghouse for Alcohol and Drug Information
P.O. Box 2345
Rockville, MD 20852
301-468-2600

National Counsel on Alcoholism
12 West 21st Street
7th Floor
New York, NY 10010
212-206-6770

National Highway Traffic Safety Administration
400 Seventh Street, SW
Washington, DC 20590
202-366-9588

National Safety Council
444 North Michigan Avenue
Chicago, IL 60611
312-527-4800

National Commission Against Drunk Driving
1140 Connecticut Ave, NW
Suite 804
Washington, DC 20036
202-452-6004

VICTIM ORGANIZATIONS

NOVA (National Organization for Victim Assistance)
1757 Park Road, NW
Washington, DC 20010
202-232-6682

National Victim Center
2111 Wilson Blvd. Suite 300
Arlington, VA 22201
703-276-2880

PUBLISHERS—Legal/Victims

NOLO Press
(self-help law books)
950 Parker Street
Berkeley, CA 94710
510-549-1976

Pathfinder Publishing of California
458 Dorothy Ave.
Ventura, CA 93003
805- 642-9278

PSYCHOLOGY/THERAPY

American Psychological Association
750 1st St., NE
Washington, DC 20006

American Association for Marriage and Family Therapy
1100 17th St., NW, 10th Floor
Washington, DC 20036
202-452-0109

National Head Injury Foundation
333 Turnpike Rd.
Southborough, MA 01772
800-444-6443

National Spinal Cord Injury Assoc.
600 W. Cummings Park, Suit 2000
Wobun, MA 01801
800-962-9629,   617-935-2722

Sunny Von Bulow Coma & Head Trauma Foundation
555 Madison Ave., Suite 32001
New York, NY 10023
212-753-5003

Appendix A

Sample Settlement Memorandum

The following is a sample cover letter and settlement memorandum that you would use in making a claim against another driver's insurance policy. Obviously this letter is to be used as a guide. You need to tailor it to fit your circumstances. For example, we do not include a section for property damage recovery; depending on your own insurance coverage and your insurer's subrogation policy, you might choose to include a property damage demand in your settlement memorandum. In the end, your memo may be longer or shorter than the sample depending on the details. The important point is to include everything and anything you feel supports your demand, but be careful not to over-dramatize. There is a fine line between realistically describing your recovery process and sounding whiny and unauthentic.

COVER LETTER

Hurt Back
0000 Empty Bank Book
El Dorado, South Dakota 20202

Date

Tough Cookie
Claims Representative
Big Bank Insurance
1234 Dead End Lane
Circular File, South Dakota 10101

Re:	Your Insured: Slow Reactions
Policy Number:	27-3-23
File Number:	007-R2D2-C3PO
Accident Date:	July 5, 19—

Dear Mr. Tough Cookie:

Enclosed is a settlement memorandum describing the facts of this case, the economic injuries caused by the accident, and the compensation required to settle this claim. Medical bills and medical reports from several medical professionals who treated my injuries, as well as wage loss verification from my employer are included as supporting documents to this claim.

I will contact you in the coming week, after you have had a chance to review these materials. I look forward to settling this case to our mutual satisfaction as soon as possible.

Sincerely,

Hurt Back

SETTLEMENT MEMORANDUM

Re: Hurt Back
Your Insured: Slow Reactions
Policy Number: 27-3-23
File Number: 007-R2D2-C3PO
Accident Date: July 5, 19—

The Accident

On July 5, 19—, I was driving through the intersection of
Lost Way Street and Look Out Avenue when your policyholder, Mr. Slow Reactions, failed to stop at his stop sign and
crashed into the passenger side of my car. The police report is
attached for your reference.

Injuries

On impact, my torso was thrown sideways, the strain focused
at my hips. Initially, I was too scared to feel anything. When I
got out of my car, my hands were shaking uncontrollably and
I had trouble concentrating. As I calmed down, my back and
sides started to stiffen up. By the time I left the accident
scene, I had a raging headache and the muscles in my lower
back were in spasm.

I was taken to Mercy Hospital for a series of spinal X-rays
and was referred to my family physician for continued treatment. A detailed diagnosis from my physician, Dr. M. Conductor, is enclosed. Dr. Conductor prescribed ongoing physical
therapy (see enclosed statement from The Feel Good Clinic)
and chiropractic treatment (see enclosed statement from Dr.
Straight Spine, D.C.), which continued for 4 months.

This treatment relieved 50-60% of the lower back pain and
stiffness caused by the accident. At this point, Dr. Conductor
concluded that the accident had seriously damaged the liga-
mentous supporting structure of my lower spine and that non-

surgical reconstructive therapy with Dr. L. Joint was required for complete recovery.

Over the following 10 months, I received this treatment while continuing with the physical therapy and chiropractic adjustments. Now, 14 months following the accident, I feel that I have fully recovered from the physical injuries I sustained.

Prior to the accident, I was extremely active, exercising 4-5 times a week. I usually worked out at a local gym three days per week, I bicycled 50 miles per week, and on the weekend I usually played volleyball, softball, or football with friends. All of this stopped the instant your policyholder ran the stop sign. The accident totally disrupted this routine and thus most of the pleasurable activities in my life. As a result of these changes, I became depressed and very frustrated. Within a week following the accident I began having violent nightmares, some exact replays of the accident. Whenever I attempted to drive or sit as a passenger in a car, I became extremely nervous and agitated. After several months of counseling, these and other disabling symptoms caused by the trauma of the accident have largely been resolved, although I doubt that I will ever feel completely safe in an automobile. I have enclosed a report from Dr. Mind Well, a clinical psychologist.

Throughout the past 14 months I have kept a journal, describing my injuries, their treatment, and the psychological ramifications of the accident experience and the lengthy recovery process required. Although I am certainly grateful to the medical professionals who helped me regain my health, when I read through this journal I find 14 months of a documented nightmare. I wouldn't wish this experience — one that I had to suffer through — on anyone.

Wage Loss

At the time of the accident, I was employed as an assistant manager with a large grocery store chain (see enclosed lost wage verification from my employer). Because of my injuries

I was unable to work for 2 months immediately following the accident and then only part-time for the next 2 months. Throughout the remainder of my recovery, I missed several more hours of work to get the ongoing medical care needed for my rehabilitation. Luckily, my time away from work has not jeopardized my career with this company.

Damage Computation

Medical Items	
Mercy Hospital	$ 750
M. Conductor, M.D.	$2,750
The Feel Good Clinic	$1,600
S. Spine, D.C.	$2,500
L. Joint, M.D.	$4,500
M. Well, Ph.D.	$3,250
Miscellaneous	$ 250
Medical Total	$15,600
Lost wages	$ 9,600
Special Damages TOTAL	$25,200

My life was seriously disrupted for several months because of the physical and emotional trauma caused by the accident. Based on this, I believe a general damage award of $20,000 is in order.

Conclusion

Given the above facts and discussion, I, Hurt Back, require forty-five thousand two hundred dollars ($45,200) to settle my claim against Slow Reactions and his insurer Big Bank Insurance.

Sincerely,

Hurt Back

ACCIDENT REPORT FORMS

DRIVER AND VEHICLE INSPECTION

Other Driver
_____

Last Name   First   Middle

Street   City   State   Zip

Home Phone   Work Phone

Driver's License No.   State   Expiration Date

Special Requirements Noted On License (e.g., corrective
lenses)

Insurance Co. Name   Policy No.   Expiration Date
__Wearing glasses__Wearing hearing aid__Wearing sunglasses
__Possibly drinking__Possibly fell asleep__Possibly ill
__Slurred speech__Obviously drunk

Coments_____
_____

Other Vehicle
_____

License Plate No.   State   Expiration Date

Make   Model   Year   Color

Safety Sticker Expiration Date
__Worn or bald tires__Headlamp burned out   __Brake lights
__Windshield clean__Flat tire __Turn signal
__Engine problem__Steering problem__Brake problem
__Windshield cracked

Describe general vehicle condition and apparent accident damage:

_____
_____
_____
_____
_____

Witnesses

Witness #1

_____
Last Name   First   Middle
_____
Street   City   State   Zip
_____
Home Phone   Work Phone
_____
Driver's License No.   State   Expiration Date
_____
License Plate No.   State   Expiration Date
_____
Make   Model   Year   Color
Comments:

_____
_____
_____
_____

Witness #2

_____
Last Name   First   Middle
_____
Street   City   State   Zip
_____
Home Phone   Work Phone
_____
Driver's License No.   State   Expiration Date
_____
License Plate No.   State   Expiration Date
_____
Make   Model   Year   Color

Comments:

_____

_____

Witness #3

_____
Last Name   First   Middle
_____
Street   City   State   Zip
_____
Home Phone   Work Phone
_____
Driver's License No.   State   Expiration Date
_____
License Plate No.   State   Expiration Date
_____
Make   Model   Year   Color
Comments:

_____

_____

_____

Physical Setting

Date and time of accident
_____
Describe the weather conditions (clear, cloudy, foggy, snow, windy, misty, etc.)

_____
Describe the lighting (dawn, dusk, twilight, hazy, grey, bright, etc.)_____

_____
Describe the traffic conditions

_____
Describe the road conditions (dry, slick, icy, paved, gravel, mud, snow, etc.)

_____

_____

Was your or the other driver's vision obscured in any way (bushes, hills, curved roadway, trees, buildings, signs, glare, other vehicles, etc.). Describe _____

_____

_____

Describe how the accident occurred

_____

_____

_____

_____

_____

_____

_____

_____

_____

_____

_____

_____

_____

Make a Sketch of the Accident

Appendix

Injuries

Note the vehicle, seating location and name and address (if possible) of those who are injured:

Injured
#1

Injured
#2

Injured
#3

Injured
#4

Note the names and badge numbers of police at the scene

Officer
#1
Officer
#2
Officer
#3
Officer
#4
Supplemental notes or comments:

INDEX

ORDER FORM

Pathfinder Publishing of California
458 Dorothy Ave.
Ventura, CA 93003
Telephone (805) 642-9278   FAX (805) 650-3656

Please send me the following books from Pathfinder Publishing:

_____Copies of **Beyond Sympathy** @ $9.95 $____
_____Copies of **Final Celebrations** @ $9.95 $____
_____Copies of **Injury** @ $12.95 $____
_____Copies of **Living Creatively**
                     With Chronic Illness @ $11.95 $____
_____Copies of **No Time For Goodbyes** @ $9.95 $____
_____Copies of **Stop Justice Abuse** @ $8.95 $____
_____Copies of **Surviving an Auto Accident** @ $12.95 $____
_____Copies of **Violence in our Schools, Hospitals and**
                     Public Places @ $22.95 Hard Cover $____
_____   @ $14.95 Soft Cover $____
_____Copies of **Violence in the Workplace** @ $22.95 Hard $____
              Violence in the Workplace @ $14.95 Soft $____
                                          Sub-Total $____
              Californians: Please add 7.25% tax. $____
              Shipping* $____
                                          Grand Total $____

I understand that I may return the book for a full refund if not satisfied.

Name:_____

Address:_____

_____ZIP:_____

*SHIPPING CHARGES U.S.
Books: Enclose $2.50 for the first book and .50c for each additional book. UPS: Truck; $4.25 for first item, .50c for each additional. UPS Air: $7.50 for first item, $.75 for each additional item.